TABLE OF CONTENTS

PREFACE

The objective of this report is to assess the scope of the problem of marijuana within the United States and its associated territories. The report attempts to determine the annual amount of marijuana available in this country, including domestically produced and imported marijuana; the major avenues through which marijuana from foreign sources is smuggled into the United States; how much of the total production actually gets seized by law enforcement authorities; and to identify links to organized crime and terrorist groups. Within the context of these objectives, this survey summarizes and assesses the most authoritative data published by the U.S. government agencies that specialize in counter-narcotics issues. Practically all of the data contained in this survey are derived from the online publications of these agencies. Such publications provide the most up-to-date information available on the subject.

This survey focuses primarily on the 50 U.S. states, but also, to the extent that data are available, on selected U.S. territories (American Samoa, Commonwealth of the Northern Mariana Islands, Guam, and the Virgin Islands), as well as the Commonwealth of Puerto Rico, which is associated with the United States. The other U.S. territories may also have a marijuana problem, but available pertinent data were insufficient to warrant their inclusion.

Most of the most publications cited in this survey are those of two agencies in particular: the U.S. Department of Justice's Drug Enforcement Administration (DEA) and the National Drug Intelligence Center (NDIC). The publications of the DEA and NDIC proved to be by far the most relevant for the purposes of this survey, which is largely a summary of their data. Unless noted otherwise, most of the data in the Appendix section on states and territories come from DEA Public Affairs, *Drug Trafficking in the United States*, July 25, 2003. The NDIC publications were particularly useful. The NDIC, which is a member of the Intelligence Community, is the nation's principal center for strategic domestic counterdrug intelligence. Several publications of the White House's Office of National Drug Control Policy (ONDCP) were also used.

This survey also incorporates some relevant statistics on foreign sources of marijuana contained in the annual *International Narcotics Control Strategy Report* (INCSR), which is published by the U.S. Department of State's Bureau for International Narcotics and Law Enforcement Affairs (INL); and the annual *Global Illicit Drug Trends* (GIDT) report, which is published by the United Nations Office on Drugs and Crime (UNODC). However, data from the

GIDT and the INCSR are cited with the caveat that they cannot be assumed to be consistently reliable. Both publications rely on foreign government reporting, and these data are often incomplete and unreliable, as is clearly the case with the data on Jamaica and Mexico. The UNODC data on U.S. marijuana cited in this survey presumably were provided by U.S. government sources, but they do not necessarily correspond with information found in the published U.S. government reports, and therefore are cited only for comparative purposes. The INCSR is considered by some analysts to be more authoritative than the GIDT. Nevertheless, a significant limitation of the usefulness of the INCSR to this survey is its conspicuous omission of data on the United States. Although providing data on domestic U.S. production of marijuana and other drugs is not within the mandate of the INCSR, marijuana cultivation and production is a major underground industry in this country.

Table A. Selected Acronyms and Abbreviations

Acronym or Abbreviation	Organization or Term
CBAG	California Border Alliance Group
CNC	Crime and Narcotics Center
CQA	Guam Customs and Quarantine Authority
CSIS	Canadian Security Intelligence Service
DCE/SP	Domestic Cannabis Eradication and Suppression Program
DEA	Drug Enforcement Administration
ELN	Ejército Nacional de Liberación (National Liberation Army)
EPIC	El Paso Intelligence Center
FARC	Fuerzas Armadas Revolucionarias de Colombia (Revolutionary Armed Forces of Colombia)
FDSS	Federal-wide Drug Seizure System
GIDT	*Global Illicit Drug Trends*
GPS	Global Positioning System
HIDTA	High Intensity Drug Trafficking Area
INCSR	*International Narcotics Control Strategy Report*
INL	Bureau for International Narcotics and Law Enforcement Affairs
JDF	Jamaica Defence Force
MAM	Marijuana Availability Model
MAWG	Marijuana Availability Working Group
MIA	Miami International Airport
NAFTA	North American Free Trade Agreement
NDIC	National Drug Intelligence Center
NDTS	National Drug Threat Survey
NHSDA	National Household Survey on Drug Abuse (now called the National Survey on Drug Use and Health (NSDUH))
NIBC	South America/Caribbean Strategic Intelligence Unit
NIDA	National Institute on Drug Abuse
NSDUH	National Survey on Drug Use and Health *(*formerly called the National Household Survey on Drug Abuse (NHSDA))
OAS	Office of Applied Studies
ONDCP	Office of National Drug Control Policy
PIJ	Palestinian Islamic Jihad
RCMP	Royal Canadian Mounted Police
SAMHSA	Department of Health and Human Services' Substance Abuse and Mental Health Services Administration
SLED	South Carolina Law Enforcement Division
STRIDE	System to Retrieve Information from Drug Evidence
THC	delta-9-tetrahydrocannabinol
UNODC	United Nations Office on Drugs and Crime
USCS	U.S. Customs Service
USPS	U.S. Postal Service
USVI	U.S. Virgin Islands

EXECUTIVE SUMMARY

Marijuana is considered by the Drug Enforcement Administration (DEA) and the National Drug Intelligence Center (NDIC) to be "a leading drug threat to the country." However, U.S. law enforcement authorities generally regard marijuana as a lower threat than cocaine and diverted pharmaceuticals because it is less often associated with violent crime and property crime. Marijuana is the most readily available and widely used and abused illicit drug in the nation. Its prevalence has contributed to both an acceptance of marijuana use among some adults and adolescents and a perception that the drug is not harmful.[1]

There is no accepted estimate for marijuana demand in the United States, but estimates of the number of users suggest that the demand for marijuana vastly exceeds demand for any other drug, especially among younger users.[2] Some national substance abuse indicators suggest that marijuana use may rise despite relatively stable levels of use since the late 1990s. The number of past-year users increased significantly in 2001, and national-level prevalence studies show some decreases in the perception of risk regarding marijuana use.

Marijuana availability has changed little since 2002, according to reporting from law enforcement and public health agencies, as well as federal investigation, arrest, and seizure data.[3] However, availability depends on the state and the type of marijuana. Seizure statistics indicate very limited availability of imported marijuana in a remote state like Alaska but significantly increasing quantities in Texas. It is also important to distinguish between the low-quality, commercial-grade marijuana imported from Mexico and the high-grade product imported from Canada. The availability of high-grade marijuana, most of which comes from Canada, is increasing in every region of the United States.[4]

In estimating the amount of marijuana available in the United States and its territories, a two-part methodology that assesses the availability of both foreign and domestically produced marijuana appears to be the most logical approach. The White House's Office of National Drug Control Policy (ONDCP) tasked the Marijuana Availability Working Group (MAWG),

---

[1] This paragraph is based on National Drug Intelligence Center (NDIC), *National Drug Threat Assessment 2003,* January 2003. [http://www.usdoj.gov/ndic/pubs3/3300/execsum.htm#Top]
[2] NDIC, *National Drug Threat Assessment 2001 - The Domestic Pers*pective, October 2000. [http://www.usdoj.gov/ndic/pubs/647/marijuan.htm#Top]
[3] National Drug Intelligence Center (NDIC), *National Drug Threat Assessment 2003,* January 2003. [http://www.usdoj.gov/ndic/pubs3/3300/execsum.htm#Top]
[4] NDIC, *National Drug Threat Assessment 2003,* January 2003.

consisting of members of various federal agencies, with developing a methodology for making a reliable estimate of the amount of marijuana available in the United States on an annual basis. Using this two-phased methodology, the MAWG calculated a speculative estimate of domestic marijuana production by applying three hypothetical seizure rates to domestic cannabis eradication figures. Based on the federal seizure of 1,215 metric tons of marijuana in 2001, the MAWG estimated the street availability of marijuana in 2001 to be between 10,000 and 24,000 pure metric tons.[5]

The data reviewed for this survey suggest that the street availability of marijuana is more likely closer to the figure of 24,000 metric tons than it is to 10,000 metric tons. There appears to some consensus that marijuana imported from Colombia and Mexico alone totals 7,500 metric tons. An undetermined but considerably smaller amount is imported from Canada and Jamaica. There is no generally accepted estimate for domestic marijuana production because of the discreet nature of cannabis cultivation, but available data suggest that marijuana production is high in the United States.[6] The United Nations Office on Drugs and Crime (UNODC) and U.S. officials have estimated that the domestic annual U.S. production of marijuana totals about 10,000 tons, and that roughly the same amount is imported. Thus, imported and domestically produced marijuana appears to total close to 20,000 tons per year. For the purpose of this general, unscientific survey, that figure provides a useful benchmark.

Cannabis is cultivated indoors and outdoors in every state and U.S. territory (for relevant marijuana data on the 50 U.S. states, the District of Columbia, and four associated U.S. territories, see Appendix). Indoor cultivation of high-grade hydroponic marijuana is increasing rapidly across the country, basically because indoor grows are less risky than outdoor grows. Independent Caucasian growers are responsible for most of the cultivation, transportation, and distribution of domestically produced marijuana, but Mexican drug-trafficking organizations are heavily involved in the cultivation, transportation, and distribution of Mexico-produced marijuana, as well as much of the cannabis being cultivated in the national forests. All of U.S. national forests are being extensively exploited and damaged by cannabis cultivators, some of whom are illegal aliens hired by Mexican drug-trafficking organizations. Marijuana growers

---

[5] This paragraph is based on ONDCP, Drug Availability Estimates in the United States, December 2002.
[6] NDIC, *United States-Canada Border Drug Threat Assessment*, December 2001.

armed with weapons such as AK-47 assault rifles have made the national parks especially dangerous for park rangers.

At most, U.S. authorities are able to seize only about 10 percent of marijuana, and most of this amount is from foreign sources of supply. According to Federal-wide Drug Seizure System (FDSS) data, Texas ranked first in the amount of marijuana seized in 2002, accounting for more than the amount confiscated in the other 49 states combined. State-by-state DEA statistics on marijuana seizures in 2002 that are listed in the Appendix appear to be greatly underestimated because they are generally sharply lower than the more authoritative FDSS statistics for the same year.

The four principal foreign sources of the U.S. marijuana supply are Mexico, Colombia, Canada, and Jamaica. Polydrug-trafficking organizations in Mexico produce most of the marijuana consumed in the United States. Most of the marijuana comes from Mexico, accounting for an estimated 7,500 tons of low-grade product smuggled annually into this country. Nearly all of Mexico's marijuana production is intended for U.S. markets. Mexican drug cartels control the smuggling, transportation, and wholesale distribution of commercial-grade Mexican marijuana. Colombian and Jamaican drug-trafficking organizations are also involved, but have a lower profile.

Drug-trafficking groups in Canada reportedly supply considerably less marijuana than either Mexico or Colombia, but most of it is extremely profitable high-grade marijuana, for which there is increasingly greater demand in the United States. Organized motorcycle gangs, particularly the Hells Angels, and Asian trafficking organizations, especially Vietnamese, are responsible for most marijuana smuggling from Canada to the United States.[7] Jamaican organized criminal groups based in Ontario control most liquid hashish trafficking through the United States to Canada.

Four principal avenues allow marijuana to flow north from Mexico through the United States and to western and eastern Canada, northeast from the Caribbean through Florida to the eastern United States and eastern Canada, and south from British Columbia in western Canada to the western and eastern United States. The Southwest border route accounts for an estimated 65 percent of illicit drugs sold in the United States, with marijuana being the most transshipped

---

[7] NDIC, *National Drug Threat Assessment 2001 - The Domestic Pers*pective, October 2000.
[http://www.usdoj.gov/ndic/pubs/647/marijuan.htm#Top]

narcotic. Transport of marijuana from source areas to markets occurs by many methods but primarily overland in commercial and private vehicles.[8] Primary market areas for marijuana include Central Arizona (Phoenix and Tucson), Chicago, Los Angeles, Miami, New York, and Seattle.[9] U.S. drug agencies assess distribution of marijuana in the United States as stable, with a wide range of criminal groups, gangs, and independent dealers distributing the drug throughout the country. Organized crime groups are becoming increasingly involved in cannabis cultivation in the United States on a large scale, often controlling or coordinating the transportation and distribution of marijuana with other criminal groups.

There has been relatively little open-source reporting on possible involvement by terrorist groups in marijuana trafficking in the United States. Afghan and Pakistani terrorist groups are known to be financed by approximately US$20 million of illicit funds derived from the sale of hashish in Canada. Indications emerged in news media in 2003 of possible Hizballah collaboration with Mexican drug cartels in the cultivation of cannabis in California's Sequoia National Park. The cannabis fields are believed to be financed by the Mexican drug cartels that dominate the methamphetamine trade in the adjacent Central Valley and, in turn, have financial ties to Middle Eastern smugglers linked to Hizballah and other terrorist groups. Apparently, the cartels are using profits from methamphetamine smuggled by Hizballah associates from Canada into California to invest in expanding marijuana growing.

---

[8] This paragraph is based in part on NDIC, *National Drug Threat Assessment 2003*, January 2003. [http://www.usdoj.gov/ndic/pubs3/3300/marijuan.htm#Top]
[9] This paragraph is based on NDIC, *National Drug Threat Assessment 2003,* January 2003.

INTRODUCTION

Products of the Cannabis Herb

Marijuana is the mind-altering substance and product of the Cannabis sativa L. plant. With certain medical exceptions, marijuana is a Schedule I substance under the Controlled Substances Act, and therefore is illegal. By far the most widely trafficked drug worldwide, marijuana is used because its primary active chemical, delta-9-tetrahydrocannabinol (THC), may induce relaxation and heighten the senses.

Cannabis resin (hashish) is also one of the most widely trafficked, illicit drugs. Hashish and hashish oil, two additional Schedule I controlled substances derived

Cannabis sativa L. plant
Source: U.S. DEA, 1999

from the cannabis plant, are in limited demand in the United States.[10] Hashish is the THC-rich resinous material from the flowering tops of the female plant; potency averages 6 percent.[11]

According to the NDIC, marijuana often is defined not by its source of origin but by its quality.[12] Lower-quality or commercial-grade marijuana usually includes all parts of the plant—the dried, shredded leaves, stems, seeds, and flowers. This grade has a low potency ranging between approximately 1 percent and 6 percent THC. Mexico-produced marijuana, which has a low THC content, is commercial-grade and relatively inexpensive.

Higher-quality marijuana often is composed only of the buds and flowering top of the plant.[13] For example, sinsemilla (Spanish for "without seed") comprises just the buds and flowering tops of unpollinated female plants, where THC is most concentrated. The potency of sinsemilla can reach levels of over 30 percent THC but more often ranges between 10 percent

---

[10] United Nations Office on Drugs and Crime (UNODC), "Trafficking in Cannabis," Chapter 1.2.4, *Global Illicit Drug Trends, 2003* (Vienna, Austria), 71. [http://www.unodc.org/pdf/report_2003-06-26_1.pdf]; and U.S. DEA, *Drug Intelligence Brief: The Cannabis Situation in the United States*, December 1999. [http://www.usdoj.gov/dea/pubs/intel/99028/99028.html]

[11] NDIC, "Marijuana Update," *Intelligence Brief: National Drug Threat Assessment*, Document ID: 2002-J0403-002, August 2002. [http://www.usdoj.gov/ndic/pubs1/1335/index.htm#Overview]

[12] This paragraph is based on NDIC, "Marijuana Update," *Intelligence Brief: National Drug Threat Assessment*, Document ID: 2002-J0403-002, August 2002. [http://www.usdoj.gov/ndic/pubs1/1335/index.htm#Overview]

[13] NDIC, U.S. Department of Justice, *Marijuana Fast Facts*, March 2003. [http://www.usdoj.gov/ndic/pubs3/3593/index.htm#What]

and 15 percent.[14] This type is typical of marijuana produced in Canada. The average marijuana yield for mature sinsemilla is approximately one-half pound per plant, compared with 1 pound per plant for commercial-grade marijuana.[15] In early 2003, the national price range for sinsemilla was between $900 and $6,000 per pound.[16]

Overall potency as characterized by THC content is rising. According to data from the Potency Monitoring Project, funded by the National Institute on Drug Abuse (NIDA), the average potency of samples of all cannabis types increased from 3.00 percent in 1991 to 5.23

percent in 2001. When categorized by type, potency generally increased from 3.09 percent to 5.01 percent for commercial-grade marijuana during the same period, but fluctuated for sinsemilla. The concentration of THC in sinsemilla averaged 10.53 percent in 1991, dipped to a low of 5.77 percent in 1993, and increased steadily to a peak of 13.38 percent in 1999 before declining to 9.10 percent in 2001.[17] Those figures indicate how dramatically the average THC content of

A cannabis plant being cultivated indoors. Once the leaves, stems, seeds, and flowers of a mature plant are dried and shredded, marijuana is the resulting product.

Source: NDIC, *Marijuana Fast Facts*, March 2003.

commercial-grade and sinsemilla marijuana has risen since 1988, when the former was 3.82 percent and the latter, 7.62 percent. The sharp increase in THC content is explained in part because of improved techniques for growing cannabis indoors.[18] Domestic cannabis growers cultivate high-potency sinsemilla because it provides a product that easily competes with other illegal drugs.[19]

According to the DEA and NDIC, marijuana, as the most readily available and widely used illicit drug in the United States, is a leading drug threat to the country. Marijuana's

---

[14] This paragraph is based in part on NDIC, *National Drug Threat Assessment 2003*, January 2003.
[15] NDIC, *West Virginia Drug Threat Assessment*, Document ID: 2003-S0379WV-001, August 2003.
[16] U.S. DEA Public Affairs, *Drug Trafficking in the United States*, July 25, 2003.
[17] NDIC, "Marijuana Update," *Intelligence Brief: National Drug Threat Assessment*, Document ID: 2002-J0403-002, August 2002. [http://www.usdoj.gov/ndic/pubs1/1335/index.htm#Overview]
[18] NDIC, *National Drug Threat Assessment 2001 - The Domestic Pers*pective, October 2000. [http://www.usdoj.gov/ndic/pubs/647/marijuan.htm#Top]
[19] U.S. DEA, *Drug Trafficking in the United States*, October 6, 2003. [http://www.usdoj.gov/dea/concern/drug_trafficking.html]

prevalence has contributed to both an acceptance of its use among some adults and adolescents and a perception that its use is not harmful and that use carries little social stigma. However, the current user population is exposed to more potent marijuana than in previous years, and strong or high doses may result in rapidly fluctuating emotions, disorientation, or hallucinations, thereby exposing users and those around them to potential harm. Marijuana used in combination with, or as a delivery medium for, other drugs further increases the risk.[20]

Popularity

The U.S. demand for marijuana is high—far exceeding that of any other illicit drug. Although this report is concerned with compiling data on marijuana production and availability in the United States and not with quantifying marijuana usage among various age groups, some basic statistics can be summarized in order to better appreciate the scope of the problem. Marijuana had an estimated 11.5 million users in 2003.[21] By 2002, an estimated 40 percent of Americans of age 12 or older had used marijuana or hashish in their lifetime.[22] Total usage figures tend to vary, however, depending on the source. For example, in 2002 the number of marijuana users in this country totaled 14.6 million, according to the National Household Survey on Drug Abuse (NHSDA).[23] Of that number, about one-third, or 4.8 million people, had used it on 20 or more days in the past month.

In 2002, 75 percent of current illicit drug users consumed marijuana.[24] Approximately 55 percent of illicit drug users in 2002 used only marijuana, 20 percent used marijuana and another illicit drug, and the remaining 25 percent used an illicit drug but not marijuana in the past month. During 2002, almost 50 percent of college students and almost 57 percent of young adults between the ages of 19 and 28 reported having used marijuana within their lifetime (see Table 1).

---

[20] NDIC, "Marijuana Update," *Intelligence Brief: National Drug Threat Assessment*, Document ID: 2002-J0403-002, August 2002. [http://www.usdoj.gov/ndic/pubs1/1335/index.htm#Overview]
[21] U.S. DEA, Public Affairs, *Drug Trafficking in the United States*, U.S. DEA, July 25, 2003. [http://www.usdoj.gov/dea/concern/drug_trafficking.html]
[22] NDIC, "Marijuana Update," *Intelligence Brief: National Drug Threat Assessment*, Document ID: 2002-J0403-002, August 2002. [http://www.usdoj.gov/ndic/pubs1/1335/index.htm#Overview]
[23] National Survey on Drug Use and Health (formerly called the National Household Survey on Drug Abuse (NHSDA), *2002 National Survey on Drug Use and Health*. [http://www.samhsa.gov/oas/nhsda.htm]; and Substance Abuse and Mental Health Services Administration (SAMHSA). (2003). *Overview of Findings from the 2002 National Survey on Drug Use and Health* (Office of Applied Studies, NHSDA Series H-21, DHHS Publication No. SMA 03–3774). Rockville, MD.
[24] SAMHSA. "Illicit Drug Use," *Results from the 2002 National Survey on Drug Use and Health: National Findings*, 2003.

Table 1. Percentage of College Students and Young Adults Reporting Marijuana Use, 2002

	Lifetime	Annual	Past 30 Days
College Students	49.5	34.7	19.7
Young Adults	56.8	29.3	16.9

Source: National Institute on Drug Abuse and University of Michigan, *Monitoring the Future National Survey Results on Drug Use, 1975–2002*, Volume II: College Students & Adults Ages 19–40 (PDF), 2003.

According to the 2002 Monitoring the Future study, 47.8 percent of 12th, 38.7 percent of 10th, and 19.2 percent of 8th graders had used marijuana in their lifetime. The 2002 study also found that 6 percent of 12th, 3.9 percent of 10th, and 1.2 percent of 8th graders had used marijuana daily in the past 30 days before the survey (see Table 2).[25]

Table 2. Percentage of High School Students Reporting Marijuana/Hashish Use, 2002

Marijuana/Hashish Use	Eighth Grade	Tenth Grade	Twelfth Grade
Daily	1.2	3.9	6.0
30-Day	8.3	17.8	21.5
Annual	14.6	30.3	36.2
Lifetime	19.2	38.7	47.8

Source: National Institute on Drug Abuse, *2002 Monitoring the Future* Data Tables: Table 1, Trends in Lifetime Prevalence (PDF); Table 2, Trends in Annual and 30-Day Prevalence (PDF); Table 3, Trends in 30-Day Prevalence of Daily Use (PDF).

National-level drug prevalence indicators show that the rates of marijuana use are higher today than in the early 1990s, when marijuana use waned.[26] The Monitoring the Future study also tracks trends in perceived risk, disapproval, and availability of drugs to youth. More than half (53 percent) of high school seniors in 2002 believed that it was harmful to smoke marijuana regularly and 78.3 percent disapproved of regular marijuana use. Since the study began in 1975,

---

[25] Office of National Drug Control Policy. *Drug Facts: Marijuana*, February 2003. http://www.whitehousedrugpolicy.gov/drugfact/marijuana/index.html. More in-depth information on marijuana usage in the United States can be found in the surveys published by the Office of Applied Studies (OAS), an Office within the Department of Health and Human Services' SAMHSA. See *Overview of Findings from the 2002 National Survey on Drug Use and Health* [http://www.samhsa.gov/oas/nhsda/2k2nsduh/Overview/2k2Overview.htm#toc]
[26] NDIC, "Marijuana Update," *Intelligence Brief: National Drug Threat Assessment*, Document ID: 2002-J0403-002, August 2002.

between 83 percent and 90 percent of every senior class have said that they could obtain marijuana fairly easy or very easily.[27]

Marijuana is popular partially as a result of popularization by the media and by groups advocating legalization, and the trend of smoking marijuana-filled cigars known as "blunts."[28] The Internet also contributes to marijuana's popularity. Marijuana appears to be the drug most commonly promoted on the Internet, and information regarding its cultivation, use, and sale is widely available.[29] Websites exist that provide information and links extolling the virtues of marijuana. These sites provide forums for user-group discussions, post documents and messages for public discussions, and advocate the "legal" sale of marijuana. Several Websites advertising the sale of marijuana and providing instructions on home grows have also been identified.

U.S. counterdrug officials consider marijuana to be a "gateway" to the world of illicit drug abuse, that is, its use results in an increased likelihood that the user will be susceptible to more serious drugs such as cocaine and heroin. However, a study by the RAND Drug Policy Research Center casts doubt on claims that marijuana acts as a "gateway" to the use of cocaine and heroin, challenging an assumption that has guided U.S. drug policies since the 1950s.[30]

Availability

According to *Pulse Check*,[31] the most available type of marijuana is domestically produced commercial-grade, followed by Mexico-produced commercial-grade, then sinsemilla.[32] As reported in the *Pulse Checks* publications of the ONDCP (Office of National Drug Control Policy), all but one of the 40 law enforcement and epidemiological/ethnographic sources consider marijuana widely available in their communities. The exception continues to be in

---

[27] National Institute on Drug Abuse, 2002 Monitoring the Future Data Tables, Table 9-Long-Term Trends in Harmfulness of Drugs as Perceived by 12th Graders (PDF), Table 11-Long-Term Trends in Disapproval of Drug Use by 12th Graders (PDF), Table 13-Long-Term Trends in Perceived Availability of Drugs, 12th Graders (PDF).
[28] This paragraph is based in part on NDIC, *National Drug Threat Assessment 2003*, January 2003; and in part on Drug Facts, "Marijuana," Office of National Drug Control Policy [http://www.whitehousedrugpolicy.gov/drugfact/marijuana/index.html]
[29] NDIC, *Information Bulletin: Drugs, Youth, and the Internet*, Document ID: 2002-L0424-006, October 2002. [http://www.usdoj.gov/ndic/pubs2/2161/index.htm]
[30] See Andrew R. Morral, Daniel F. McCaffrey, and Susan M. Paddock, "Reassessing the Marijuana Gateway Effect," *Addiction*, Vol 97, 2002: 1493-1504.
[31] *Pulse Check* is a biannual, multijurisdictional publication of the ONDCP that describes current trends in illicit drug use and drug markets based on nationwide interviews conducted with ethnographers and epidemiologists, law enforcement officials, and drug treatment providers. It is available at: <http://www.whitehousedrugpolicy.gov/drugfact/pulsecheck.html>.
[32] This paragraph is based in part on NDIC, *National Drug Threat Assessment 2003*, January 2003.

Chicago, where a law enforcement source considers the drug somewhat available.[33] This is a puzzling exception because Chicago is generally considered to be a major hub for transshipping marijuana, as well as a primary destination for the drug. Primary market areas for marijuana include Central Arizona, Chicago, Los Angeles, Miami, New York, and Seattle.[34] New York City and Miami are the key wholesale-level drug distribution centers[35] on the East Coast and major drug-importation hubs (see Figure 1).[36]

Most state and local law enforcement agencies that responded to the National Drug Threat Survey (NDTS) 2001 of the NDIC identified marijuana availability and use in the United States as high, while identifying the threat of marijuana to public safety and health as stable at varying levels.[37] NDTS data show that 96.9 percent of state and local law enforcement agencies nationwide describe the availability of marijuana as high or medium; only 1.8 percent describes it as low. From region to region, the proportions of agencies reporting high or medium

availability were very similar and ranged only from 98.9 percent in the Mid-Atlantic region to 91.6 percent in the Florida/Caribbean.[38]

According to NDTS data, the identification of marijuana as the principal drug threat varies from region to region. Marijuana is identified as more of a

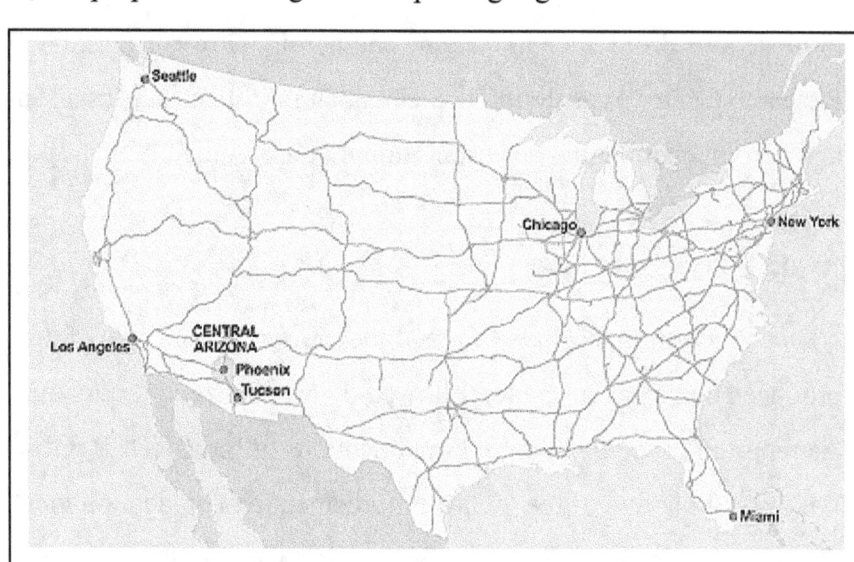

Figure 1. Primary U.S. Market Areas for Marijuana

Source: National Drug Intelligence Center (NDIC), January 2003

threat in the following regions: New York/New Jersey (40.9 percent), Great Lakes (29.6 percent), New England (27.3 percent), Mid-Atlantic (21.0 percent), and Southwest (19.7

---

[33] "Marijuana," *Pulse Check*: Trends in Drug Abuse, Executive Office of the President, Office of National Drug Control Policy, November 2002. [http://www.whitehousedrugpolicy.gov/publications/drugfact/pulsechk/]
[34] This paragraph is based in part on NDIC, *National Drug Threat Assessment 2003*, January 2003.
[35] A distribution center is a city or area in the United States that regularly receives wholesale quantities of drugs from a domestic source and supplies wholesale or midlevel quantities to markets in and out of state.
[36] U.S. DEA *Briefs and Background*, "Georgia," http://www.usdoj.gov/dea/pubs/states/georgia.html.
[37] This paragraph is based in part on NDIC, *National Drug Threat Assessment 2003*, January 2003.
[38] This paragraph is based in part on NDIC, *National Drug Threat Assessment 2003*, January 2003.

percent). It is identified as less of a threat in the following regions: Florida/Caribbean (10.9 percent), West Central (9.9 percent), Southeast (9.3 percent), and Pacific (7.8 percent).[39]

Of the two most common varieties of marijuana—local commercial grade and Mexican commercial grade—the former is ranked as widely available by 23 sources in all but four of the *Pulse Check* cities (Boston, Chicago, Detroit, and El Paso); the latter grade is ranked as such by 21 sources in all but three cities (Miami, Portland, and Washington, D.C.).[40] Sinsemilla (seedless marijuana) remains the third most common variety (ranked widely available by 16 sources in 12 cities), followed by hydroponically grown marijuana (ranked widely available by 12 sources in nine cities). British Columbian marijuana (BC Bud) remains the least common variety, with only six sources ranking it as widely available in four cities: Baltimore, Billings, New York, and Seattle.[41] It is also popular in the affluent Boston area.

DOMESTICALLY PRODUCED MARIJUANA

An important source for marijuana in the United States is domestically grown cannabis, which includes both indoor and outdoor operations.[42] U.S. drug law enforcement reporting suggests increased availability of domestically grown marijuana.[43] The Appalachian Mountain region—which includes portions of Tennessee, Kentucky, and West Virginia—is considered one of the most productive cannabis-growing regions in the country.[44]

In 2002, the DEA's Domestic Cannabis Eradication and Suppression Program (DCE/SP), a DEA program that supports 88 state and local law enforcement agencies, reported that a total of 3,341,840 indoor and outdoor cannabis plants were eradicated.[45] Although this statistic does not indicate the total estimated amount of marijuana in the United States, it provides an indicator

---

[39] This paragraph is based in part on NDIC, *National Drug Threat Assessment 2003*, January 2003.
[40] "Marijuana," *Pulse Check*: Trends in Drug Abuse, Office of National Drug Control Policy, November 2002. [http://www.whitehousedrugpolicy.gov/publications/drugfact/pulsechk/]
[41] "Marijuana," *Pulse Check*: Trends in Drug Abuse, Office of National Drug Control Policy, November 2002. [http://www.whitehousedrugpolicy.gov/publications/drugfact/pulsechk/]
[42] ONDCP, *Drug Facts*, "Marijuana," Office of National Drug Control Policy [http://www.whitehousedrugpolicy.gov/drugfact/marijuana/index.html]
[43] U.S. DEA Public Affairs, *Drug Trafficking in the United States*, July 25, 2003.
[44] NDIC, *Tennessee Drug Threat Assessment Update*, May 2002. [http://www.usdoj.gov/ndic/pubs1/1017/marijuan.htm#Top]
[45] This paragraph is based on NDIC, "Marijuana Update," *Intelligence Brief: National Drug Threat Assessment*, Document ID: 2002-J0403-002, August 2002; and U.S. Department of Justice, Drug Enforcement Administration, *Sourcebook of Criminal Justice Statistics Online*, Table 4.38. [http://www.albany.edu/sourcebook/1995/pdf/t438.pdf].

of the general prevalence of cannabis herb, without even taking into account that an estimated 50 percent of the marijuana available in the United States is imported. U.S. authorities estimate that approximately 10,000 tons of marijuana are produced domestically in the United States.[46]

Whether cultivated indoors or outdoors, most domestically produced marijuana is intended for sale and use in the local area.[47] Some of the marijuana produced in the high-production states (Alabama, Alaska, California, Florida, Hawaii, Kentucky, Oregon, and Tennessee) undoubtedly is transported to other areas for sale. State and local law enforcement agencies throughout the United States identify Chicago and New York most frequently as destinations for marijuana transshipped through their areas.

Indoor Domestic Grows

Indoor growing operations are becoming a large-scale problem. According to 2000 DCE/SP statistics of the DEA, the five leading states for indoor growing activity were California, Florida, Oregon, Washington, and Wisconsin.[48] This listing differs slightly from the Bureau of Justice statistics, which lists the five leading states for indoor growing activity as California, Washington, Florida, Texas, and Alaska.[49] These states

Indoor cultivation of marijuana

Source: U.S. DEA, 1999

do not necessarily have the most cannabis, but they may have the most, or the most effective, eradication programs.

Eradication programs and drought conditions in some states have led many growers to abandon outdoor cultivation for indoor sites, which allow growers to better conceal their

---

[46] United Nations Office on Drugs and Crime (UNODC), "Trafficking in Cannabis," Chapter 1.2.4, *Global Illicit Drug Trends, 2003* (Vienna, Austria), 72. [http://www.unodc.org/pdf/report_2003-06-26_1.pdf]

[47] The rest of this paragraph is based on NDIC, *National Drug Threat Assessment 2001 - The Domestic Pers*pective, October 2000.

[48] U.S. DEA Public Affairs, *Drug Trafficking in the United States*, July 25, 2003. [http://www.usdoj.gov/dea/pubs/intel/01020/index.html#ma1]

[49] Bureau of Justice Statistics, *Sourcebook of Criminal Justice Statistics 2000*, Table 4.38, December 2001.

operations and to control the growing environment. Financial benefits also have encouraged growers to move their operations indoors. Automated systems that can monitor and manipulate conditions in the grow room and advanced growing techniques such as hydroponics have raised not only the quality of the marijuana produced but also the profits derived from its sale.[50] Hydroponic grow operations have been identified in every state and in Puerto Rico.[51] (The high-grade marijuana produced in hydroponic operations is often called 'hydro.")

Outdoor Domestic Grows

According to preliminary 2000 DEA reporting, outdoor growing operations are large-scale problems in many states.[52] DCE/SP statistics corroborate that the major outdoor growing states in 2000 and 2001 continued to be California, Hawaii, Kentucky, and Tennessee. As they have since at least 1998, these states accounted for over 75 percent of the total of eradicated outdoor cultivated plants, according to 1998 DEA eradication statistics.[53] DEA statistics also show that 3,068,632 outdoor cultivated cannabis plants were eradicated in the United States during 2001 (see Table 3, Appendix).

The 10 Most Dangerous National Parks for Rangers:

1. Organ Pipe Cactus National Monument (Arizona)
2. Amistad National Recreation Area (Texas)
3. Big Bend National Park (Texas)
4. Lake Mead National Recreation Area (Nevada/Arizona)
5. Coronado National Memorial (Arizona)
6. Biscayne National Park (Florida)
7. Shenandoah National Park (Virginia)
8. Delaware Water Gap (New Jersey/Pennsylvania)
9. Edison National Historic Site (New Jersey)
10. Yellowstone National Park (Wyoming)

Source: Source: U.S Park Rangers Lodge of the Fraternal Order of Police, October 2003

Outdoor cannabis growers often conceal plants in an effort to avoid detection by law enforcement authorities. Cannabis cultivators often scatter the plants among other crops, use camouflage netting, and establish cultivation sites in remote wooded locations. Federal, state, and local agencies also continue to identify the widespread use of public lands for the cultivation

---

[50] This paragraph derives from NDIC, "Marijuana Update," Intelligence Brief: National Drug Threat Assessment, Document ID: 2002-J0403-002, August 2002.

[51] This paragraph is based on NDIC, "Marijuana Update," *Intelligence Brief: National Drug Threat Assessment*, Document ID: 2002-J0403-002, August 2002. [http://www.usdoj.gov/ndic/pubs1/1335/index.htm#Overview]

[52] U.S. DEA Public Affairs, *Drug Trafficking in the United States*, July 25, 2003.

[53] U.S. DEA Public Affairs, *Drug Trafficking in the United States*, July 25, 2003; and Bureau of Justice Statistics, *Sourcebook of Criminal Justice Statistics 2000*, Table 4.38, December 2001. These states do not necessarily have the most cannabis, but they may have the most, or the most effective, eradication programs.

of cannabis. In 1999, the U.S. Forest Service seized almost 1 million pounds of cannabis plants and processed marijuana in 35 states. California led all states with more than 500,000 pounds seized, followed by Kentucky (474,300 pounds), Utah (19,300 pounds), North Carolina (14,600 pounds), and Washington (10,300 pounds).

Many of the key outdoor cultivation areas in the United States are on national forestland (see Table 4). Along with ideal growing conditions, timber practices in the national forests have opened a canopy for new marijuana growth in numerous areas where the sunlight penetrates the forest floor. As a result, marijuana plots in the national forests are found in various locations from bottomlands, on hillsides, to the tops of mountains, with the regeneration areas being an especially popular spot for growers. Marijuana growers also perceive the vast rural areas of the national forests as too spacious for law enforcement officials to detect all activities. Aside from ideal locations for marijuana plots, growers often plant their crops on public lands, such as national forests, in an effort to draw greater protection from personal and/or financial loss from asset forfeiture procedures, should they be apprehended. The Daniel Boone National Forest in Kentucky has traditionally had the most cannabis eradicated, but according to the U.S. Forest Service, eradication numbers are surging for forests in California. Of 719,985 cannabis plants eradicated from national forestland in 2001, 495,536 were in California.[54]

As a result of the greatly increased cultivation of U.S. forests by cannabis growers, a 2003 study by the Justice Department found that park rangers are 15 times more likely to be killed or injured on the job than is an agent with the DEA.[55] In 2003, the U.S. Park Rangers Lodge of the Fraternal Order of Police listed two Texas parks—Amistad National Recreation Area near Del Rio and Big Bend National Park—among the 10 most dangerous parks in the United States for park rangers.

---

[54] U.S. Congress, House of Representatives. "Statement of Frank Deckert, Superintendent, Big Bend National Park Service, Department of the Interior, Before the House Government Reform Subcommittee on Criminal Justice, Drug Policy, and Human Resources, Regarding the Impact of the Drug Trade on Border Security and National Parks, April 15, 2003." [http://www.nps.gov/legal/testimony/108th/lebigben.htm]

[55] "Park Rangers Facing More Danger on Job: Heightened Security Near Border Places Many National Law Enforcers on Front Lines," *Houston Chronicle*, October 19, 2003, A-44; and Ralph Vartabedian, "Law Loses Out at U.S. Parks; Rangers Say They Aren't Equipped to Cope with Illegal Immigrants, Armed Smugglers," *Los Angeles Times*, January 23, 2003: A1.

U.S. Forest Service data and law enforcement reporting suggest that in California both the size of grow sites and the number of plants per site are increasing, and there is evidence of long-term occupancy of some cultivation sites by members or employees of Mexican drug-trafficking organizations. In the eastern United States, grow sites tend to be smaller, with fewer plants per site; however, the number of cultivation sites are increasing, and growers tend to travel long distances from their homes to sites scattered throughout remote areas.[56]

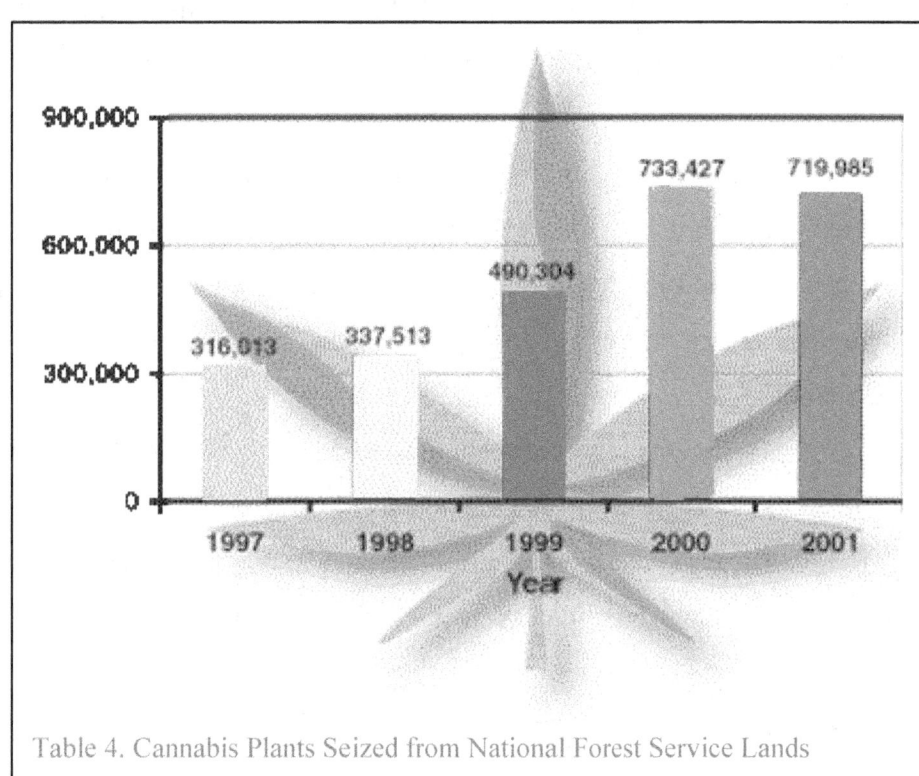

Table 4. Cannabis Plants Seized from National Forest Service Lands
Source: U.S. Forest Service, Law Enforcement and Investigations, 2001.

SOURCES OF FOREIGN-PRODUCED MARIJUANA

According to the DEA, marijuana smuggled into the United States accounts for most of the marijuana available in this country, but other official U.S. sources estimate that U.S. production accounts for at least half of the marijuana available in the nation.[57] Canada, Colombia, Jamaica, and Mexico are four principal foreign sources of marijuana in the United States.[58]

There are no conclusive data on the amount of marijuana produced in Mexico, Colombia, Canada, and Jamaica, but most appears to be produced in Mexico (7,400 metric tons in 2001, according to accepted interagency methodology). U.S. authorities estimate that more than 5,000

---

[56] The remainder of this paragraph is based on NDIC, "Marijuana Update," *Intelligence Brief: National Drug Threat Assessment*, Document ID: 2002-J0403-002, August 2002.
[57] U.S. DEA Public Affairs, *Drug Trafficking in the United States*, July 25, 2003.
[58] NDIC, United States-Canada Border Drug Threat Assessment, December 2001.

tons of marijuana are imported annually into the United States from Mexico and Canada.[59] However, that figure appears to be too low because all of the Mexican production of marijuana goes to the United States. Drug-trafficking organizations in Colombia and Mexico produce an estimated 10,000 metric tons of marijuana yearly; approximately 7,500 metric tons of that marijuana is intended for U.S. markets.

Sources in Colombia and Jamaica supply marijuana more in the eastern United States, specifically in the Southeast and New York/New Jersey regions. Marijuana supplied by both Colombian and Jamaican sources has been identified in the New England and Great Lakes regions as well, and marijuana from Jamaican sources also has been identified in the Mid-Atlantic.[60]

Traffickers in foreign source areas and in the United States supply users with large amounts of marijuana of varying potency. Lower-potency marijuana, much of which is produced in Mexico, is prevalent and is available even in major domestic cultivation areas. The prevalence of higher-potency marijuana is increasing, however.[61]

Canada

Canada increasingly is becoming a source country for high-grade marijuana smuggled into the United States.[62] High-grade marijuana smuggled into the United States from British Columbia, with a potency of 15 percent to 25 percent THC, is commonly referred to as "BC Bud," while such marijuana produced in Quebec is called "Quebec Gold."[63] Law enforcement

---

[59] United Nations Office on Drugs and Crime (UNODC), "Trafficking in Cannabis," Chapter 1.2.4, *Global Illicit Drug Trends, 2003* (Vienna, Austria), 72. [http://www.unodc.org/pdf/report_2003-06-26_1.pdf]

[60] NDIC, "Marijuana Update," Intelligence Brief: National Drug Threat Assessment, Document ID: 2002-J0403-002, August 2002. [http://www.usdoj.gov/ndic/pubs1/1335/index.htm#Overview]

[61] NDIC, "Marijuana Update," *Intelligence Brief: National Drug Threat Assessment*, Document ID: 2002-J0403-002, August 2002.

[62] This paragraph is based on U.S. DEA, *Drug Trafficking in the United States*, September 2001; NDIC, U.S. Department of Justice, *United States-Canada Border Drug Threat Assessment*, December 2001 [http://www.usdoj.gov/ndic/pubs07/794/marijuan.htm#Map%201]; and NDIC, "Marijuana Update," Intelligence Brief: National Drug Threat Assessment, Document ID: 2002-J0403-002, August 2002. [http://www.usdoj.gov/ndic/pubs1/1335/index.htm#Overview]

[63]Bureau for International Narcotics and Law Enforcement Affairs, U.S. Department of State, "Colombia," *International Narcotics Control Strategy Report, 2002*, March 2003. [http://www.state.gov/g/inl/rls/nrcrpt/2002/html/17944.htm; and U.S. DEA Public Affairs, *Drug Trafficking in the United States*, July 25, 2003. The term "BC Bud," which originally referred to the bud of the unpollinated female cannabis plant grown in British Columbia, has become synonymous with any high-grade marijuana from Canada.

and anecdotal reporting suggests that marijuana from Canada is now in every region of the United States to varying degrees.

Marijuana from Canada probably accounts for a greater proportion of available supplies in the Pacific and West Central regions than in the rest of the country, but quantities are still not as high as marijuana grown domestically or in Mexico. Although official Canadian production statistics for marijuana are unavailable, the Royal Canadian Mounted Police (RCMP) has estimated annual production of marijuana in Canada in 2001 at 800 metric tons, much of which is consumed in Canada.[64]

The primary growing area for cannabis in Canada is British Columbia, although production has spread since the mid-1990s to the eastern provinces of Ontario and Quebec. Cannabis cultivation also has increased in other Canadian provinces.

The size of cannabis grow operations in Canada varies widely, from a few plants grown in a closet to several thousand plants hidden in warehouses or underground bunkers. Canadian law enforcement intelligence indicates that marijuana traffickers there are increasingly cultivating cannabis indoors.[65] Such indoor-grow operations have become an enormous and lucrative illicit industry, producing the potent form of marijuana (BC Bud).[66] The RCMP reports that Vietnamese crime groups may have mastered organic methods of indoor cultivation of high THC-level cannabis that rival the more technical hydroponic systems.[67]

Detroit authorities seized this 3,700-pound load of marijuana on delivery to a home in the upscale community of Grosse Pointe Park, Michigan, on March 1, 2003.

Source: DEA

Canadian officials estimate that cannabis cultivation in British Columbia is a billion-dollar industry, and that traffickers smuggle a significant portion of the Canadian harvest into the United States. BC Bud sells for between US$1,500 and US$2,000 per pound in Vancouver; but when smuggled into the United States, it sells for between US$5,000 and US$8,000 per pound in major metropolitan areas.

---

[64] Bureau for International Narcotics and Law Enforcement Affairs, *International Narcotics Control Strategy Report, 2002*, March 2003; and NDIC, *United States-Canada Border Drug Threat Assessment*, December 2001.
[65] U.S. DEA Public Affairs, *Drug Trafficking in the United States*, July 25, 2003.
[66] U.S. DEA, *Drug Trafficking in the United States*, September 2001.
[67] Bureau for International Narcotics and Law Enforcement Affairs, U.S. Department of State, "Colombia," *International Narcotics Control Strategy Report, 2002*, March 2003.
[http://www.state.gov/g/inl/rls/nrcrpt/2002/html/17944.htm]

Large indoor grow operations with thousands of plants are not uncommon. In most cases, these operations are under the purview of organized crime and are often sophisticated and highly automated. Canadian cannabis cultivators, both organized groups and independent growers, appear to be opting more frequently for indoor operations because they allow for year-round cultivation and offer better protection from law enforcement and poachers. Rental properties are preferred locations.[68]

As a result of market saturation in British Columbia, an estimated 75 percent to 85 percent of the BC Bud crop in excess of a billion dollars moves to the U.S. market, using Washington State as the primary staging area to continue movement of the product to states as far as Florida.[69] A number of international publications have reported that approximately 50 percent to 60 percent of the marijuana produced in Canada is smuggled into the United States annually.[70] According to Royal Canadian Mounted Police (RCMP) officials, 95 percent of all marijuana grown in Vancouver is sent to the United States.[71] However, these estimates have not been substantiated through current reporting. The amount of marijuana seized at ports of entry along the U.S.-Canada border increased from 0.35 metric tons in FY 1999 to 3.25 metric tons in FY 2000.[72] Nevertheless, marijuana transported from Canada clearly amounts to only a small percentage of all marijuana smuggled into the United States.[73]

Colombia

Estimates of marijuana production in Colombia, while not precise, have been reported in the INCSR (*International Narcotics Control Strategy Report*) as stable at 4,150 metric tons annually since 1996 (see Table 5). There are no current accepted interagency estimates of the amount of marijuana destined for the United States from Colombia. Seizure and law enforcement reporting suggests that multi-metric-ton quantities reach U.S. markets yearly.

---

[68] NDIC, *United States-Canada Border Drug Threat Assessment*, December 2001.
[69] Office of National Drug Control Policy, Northwest HIDTA, "Northwest HIDTA: Washington," *High-Intensity Drug Trafficking Areas*, March 13, 2003. <http://www.whitehousedrugpolicy.gov/hidta/frames_nw.html>
[70] NDIC, *United States-Canada Border Drug Threat Assessment*, December 2001.
[71] Bill Curry, with files from Carl Hanlon, Global National, "U.S. Warns Pot Plan to Clog Border; Drug Czar Accuses Liberals of Naive 'Cheech and Chong' Notion of Dangers of Marijuana," *National Post* [Internet Version-www], December 11, 2002, as transcribed by FBIS Document ID: EUP20021213000341, "Canadian-US Border Views on Fingerprinting, Marijuana Decriminalization Discussed," December 13, 2002.
[72] NDIC, *United States-Canada Border Drug Threat Assessment*, December 2001.
[73] NDIC, United States-Canada Border Drug Threat Assessment, December 2001.

Table 5. Colombia Statistics on Cannabis Herb Production, Eradication, and Seizures, 1993-2002* (in metric tons)										
Year	2002	2001	2000	1999	1998	1997	1996	1995	1994	1993
Potential Harvest	5,000	5,000	5,000	5,000	5,000	5,000	5,000	4,980	4,986	5,000
Eradication	—	—	—	—	—	—	—	20	14	50
Estimated Cultivation	5,000	5,000	5,000	5,000	5,000	5,000	5,000	5,000	5,000	5,050
Potential Yield	4,150	4,150	4,150	4,150	4,150	4,150	4,150	4,133	4,138	4,125
Seizures**	73	80	46	65	69	136	235	166	2000	549

Source: Bureau for International Narcotics and Law Enforcement Affairs, U.S. Department of State, "Colombia," *International Narcotics Control Strategy Report, 2002*, March 2003. [http://www.state.gov/g/inl/rls/nrcrpt/2002/html/17944.htm]
*Reported cannabis cultivation has not been confirmed by U.S. government survey.
**Seizure data show combined Colombian National Police and military figures.

Jamaica

Jamaica is the largest producer and exporter of marijuana in the Caribbean.[74] There is no accurate estimate of the amount of cannabis under cultivation or the number of harvests per year. During 2002, the Jamaican government eradicated only 79.28 hectares of cannabis, far short of the eradication goal of 1,200 hectares agreed to in the Letter of Agreement between Jamaica and the United States under which the United States is providing counter-narcotics assistance to Jamaica (see Table 6). As a matter of policy, Jamaica does not use herbicides to eradicate cannabis. Manual cutting is the primary eradication method. In 2002, the Jamaican government seized 26,630 kilograms of marijuana and 497 kilograms of hashish oil. The Jamaican government requested U.S aerial surveillance support for a major cannabis eradication operation that was scheduled for 2003.

According to the INCSR, the last estimate of marijuana production in Jamaica was in 1997; approximately 214 metric tons were produced in that year. There are no accepted

---

[74]This paragraph is based on Bureau for International Narcotics and Law Enforcement Affairs, U.S. Department of State, "Jamaica," *International Narcotics Control Strategy Report, 2002*, March 2003. [http://www.state.gov/g/inl/rls/nrcrpt/2002/html/17944.htm]

interagency estimates of how much marijuana from Jamaica is destined for the United States. Current law enforcement information indicates, however, that marijuana from Jamaica is being smuggled in the Caribbean, often through the Bahamas, with increasing frequency.[75]

Table 6. Jamaica Statistics on Cannabis Herb Production, Eradication, and Seizures, 1993–2002										
Year	2002	2001	2000	1999	1998	1997	1996	1995	1994	1993
Potential Harvest (ha**)	Unk*	unk	unk	unk	Unk	317	527	305	308	744
Eradication (ha)	80	332	517	894	705	743	473	695	692	456
Cultivation (ha)	Unk	unk	unk	unk	unk	1,060	1,000	1,000	1,000	1,200
Potential Yield[1] (mt***)	Unk	unk	unk	unk	unk	214	356	206	208	502
Seizures[2] (mt)	26.63	68.46	55.87	56.22	35.91	24.00	52.99	37.20	46.00	75.00

[1]Yield is based on an estimate of 675 kilograms per hectare.
[2]Data derived from official information supplied by the Narcotics Division, Jamaica Constabulary Force (JCF), except for hectares of cannabis cultivation, which is based on joint estimates from the JCF, Jamaica Defence Force (JDF), and the U.S. Drug Enforcement Administration (DEA.).
*unk=unknown
**ha=hectares
***mt=metric tons

Source: Based on information from Bureau for International Narcotics and Law Enforcement Affairs, U.S. Department of State, "Jamaica," *International Narcotics Control Strategy Report, 2002*, March 2003.

Mexico

Mexico is the primary foreign supplier of marijuana to the United States, and has been a supplier of marijuana to this country for several decades.[76] Marijuana produced in Mexico is the most widely available in the United States. Nearly all marijuana produced in Mexico is likely intended for markets in the United States. Mexico produces an estimated 7,000 to 8,000 tons of marijuana annually, according to U.S. estimates (see Table 7).[77] Marijuana produced in Mexico

---

[75] This paragraph derives from NDIC, "Marijuana Update," *Intelligence Brief: National Drug Threat Assessment*, Document ID: 2002-J0403-002, August 2002.

[76] U.S. DEA, *Drug Trafficking in the United States*, September 2001; and U.S. DEA, *Drug Intelligence Brief: The Cannabis Situation in the United States*, December 1999. [http://www.usdoj.gov/dea/pubs/intel/99028/99028.html]

[77] NDIC, "Marijuana Update," Intelligence Brief: National Drug Threat Assessment, Document ID: 2002-J0403-002, August 2002; and "Mexico Country Brief," *Drug Intelligence Brief*, July 2002, U.S. DEA, citing U.S.

provides a significant supplement to that grown by domestic cultivators in the United States.

Cannabis is cultivated in small fields in remote areas of every state in Mexico, with more than 70

percent of the total cannabis crop concentrated in northwestern Mexico.[78]

Table 7. Mexico Statistics on Cannabis Herb Production, Eradication, and Seizures, 1993-2002*
(in metric tons)

Year	2002	2001	2000	1999	1998	1997	1996	1995	1994	1993
Potential Harvest	7,900	4,100	3,900	3,700	4,600	4,800	6,500	6,900	10,550	11,220
U.S. Government Estimated Impact	—	7,400	13,000	19,400	9,500	10,500	12,200	11,750	8,495	9,970
Eradication	—	33,300	33,000	33,583	23,928	23,576	22,961	21,573	14,227	16,645
Estimated Cultivation	—	11,500	16,900	23,100	14,100	15,300	18,700	18,650	19,045	21,190
Potential Yield	7,900	7,400	7,000	6,700	8,300	8,600	11,700	12,400	5,908	6,283
Seizures	1.494	2,007	1,619	1,459	1,062	1,038	1,015	780	528	495

Source: Bureau for International Narcotics and Law Enforcement Affairs, U.S. Department of State,
"Colombia," *International Narcotics Control Strategy Report, 2002*, March 2003.
[http://www.state.gov/g/inl/rls/nrcrpt/2002/html/17944.htm]

Southeast Asia

The availability of marijuana from Southeast Asia generally is limited to the West

Coast.[79] Marijuana produced in Thailand is available in limited quantities in areas of the western

United States and also in New York City.[80]

ESTIMATING MARIJUANA AVAILABILITY IN THE UNITED STATES AND ITS TERRITORIES

This report surveys the most authoritative, national-level estimates developed by federal

law enforcement, intelligence, and health-related communities and attempts to synthesize the

often inconsistent figures into a coherent, albeit wide-ranging, estimate. Any estimate is

---

Government Cultivation & Production Estimate, 2001; and United Nations Office on Drugs and Crime (UNODC),
"Cannabis," Chapter 1.1.4, *Global Illicit Drug Trends, 2003* (Vienna, Austria), 29, citing *International Narcotics
Control Strategy Report* (INCSR), March 2003. [http://www.unodc.org/pdf/report_2003-06-26_1.pdf]
[78] "Mexico Country Brief," *Drug Intelligence Brief*, July 2002, U.S. DEA.
[http://www.dea.gov/pubs/intel/02035/02035.html]
[79] U.S. DEA Public Affairs, *Drug Trafficking in the United States*, July 25, 2003.
[80] NDIC, "Marijuana Update," *Intelligence Brief: National Drug Threat Assessment*, Document ID: 2002-J0403-
002, August 2002. [http://www.usdoj.gov/ndic/pubs1/1335/index.htm#Overview]

necessarily uncertain and imprecise, however, because of the illicit and clandestine nature of marijuana and the limited data available on which to base an estimate.

No exact estimates of the amount of marijuana available in the United States have been made, and there are no reliable estimates for domestic production.[81] The widespread, clandestine cultivation and production of marijuana at indoor and outdoor sites in the United States and the lack of cannabis cultivation monitoring systems and surveys make it impossible to have an accurate assessment of the location and extent of cultivation and production. Drug-trafficking organizations in four countries—Mexico, Colombia, Canada, and Jamaica—supply most of the foreign-produced marijuana available in the United States. Thus, the only data that can provide limited insight into marijuana availability are eradication and seizure statistics.

The ONDCP (Office of National Drug Control Policy) tasked the Marijuana Availability Working Group (MAWG) with developing a methodology for making a reliable estimate of the amount of marijuana available in the United States annually.[82] The MAWG, made up of members of various federal agencies, labeled its two-part methodology the Marijuana Availability Model (MAM). Using its MAM, the MAWG calculated a speculative estimate of domestic marijuana production by applying three hypothetical seizure rates to domestic cannabis eradication figures. In calculating the availability of domestically produced marijuana, the MAWG relied on cannabis eradication statistics along with plant yield estimates (for figures of this nature, see Table 8, Appendix). The lack of direct information on the magnitude of the domestic production component created considerable uncertainty in the estimate.

In estimating the quantity of foreign-produced marijuana, the MAWG relied on a two-step approach. First, it estimated marijuana production in Mexico on the basis of data developed by the Crime and Narcotics Center (CNC) along with seizure statistics, both foreign and domestic. Second, it estimated the availability of foreign-produced marijuana from other source countries based on a calculation of the effectiveness of U.S. Customs Service (USCS) enforcement efforts against shipments of marijuana produced in Mexico. The MAWG determined that the quantity of foreign-produced marijuana available in the United States in 2001 was at least 4,581 metric tons and as high as 7,135 metric tons. Although the quantity of domestically produced marijuana available in the United States in 2001 was unknown, the

---

[81] NDIC, *National Drug Threat Assessment 2001 - The Domestic Per*spective, October 2000.
[82] This paragraph is based on ONDCP, *Drug Availability Estimates in the United States*, December 2002, x-xi, 103-04. [http://www.whitehousedrugpolicy.gov/publications/drugfact/drug_avail/index.html]

MAWG calculated—on the basis of cannabis eradication figures and potential yield per cannabis plant—that the estimated figure was between 5,577 and 16,731 metric tons. Using its two estimates derived for foreign- and domestically produced marijuana, the MAWG estimated the street availability of marijuana in 2001 to be between 10,000 and 24,000 pure metric tons.

PERCENTAGE OF TOTAL PRODUCTION SEIZED BY LAW ENFORCEMENT

Annual seizure statistics provide an important indicator of the total amount of marijuana available in the United States in a given year. Marijuana seizures reflected in the Federal-wide Drug Seizure System (FDSS) rose from 1,777,434 kilograms in 1998 to a record 2,674,826 pounds in 2001 (see Table 9 and Table 10). Seizures of marijuana reported in the FDSS show that the amount of marijuana seized declined between 2000 and 2001 from 1,236 metric tons to 1,215 metric tons.[83] It should be noted that the state-by-state DEA statistics on marijuana seizures in 2002 that are listed in the Appendix are generally sharply lower than the FDSS statistics for the same year, and therefore the DEA seizure data are most likely greatly underestimated and of dubious value.

Texas, Arizona, California, and, to a much lesser extent, New Mexico accounted for just over 90 percent (1,104 of 1,215 metric tons) of the marijuana seized in 2001; Texas alone accounted for more than half.[84] Texas ranked first nationwide in the amount of marijuana seized by federal officers in 2002. According to FDSS data, the total amount of marijuana seized in Texas in 2002 (555,324 kilograms) was greater than the amount seized in the other 49 states combined (approximately 488,000 kilograms).[85]

There seems to be general agreement among law enforcement officials that only a maximum of 10 percent of the marijuana being smuggled into the United States is intercepted. The logistics of intercepting any smuggled drugs are daunting. For example, the 10 customs inspectors at the port of Charleston—the second-largest containerized seaport on the eastern seaboard of the United States—are able to inspect fewer than 1 percent of the 1.5 million

---

[83] U.S. DEA, *Drug Trafficking in the United States*, September 2001; NDIC, "Marijuana Update," *Intelligence Brief: National Drug Threat Assessment*, Document ID: 2002-J0403-002, August 2002 [http://www.usdoj.gov/ndic/pubs1/1335/index.htm#Overview]; and U.S. DEA Public Affairs, *Drug Trafficking in the United States*, July 25, 2003.
[84] This paragraph is based in part on NDIC, *National Drug Threat Assessment 2003*, January 2003.
[85] NDIC, *Texas Drug Threat Assessment*, Document ID: 2003-S0387TX-001, October 2003. [http://www.usdoj.gov/ndic/pubs5/5624/index.htm]

containers that pass through the port annually. The DEA estimates that for every container loaded with illegal drugs discovered at the Charleston port, at least nine other containers with illegal drugs have slipped through without detection.[86]

Calculating the total amount of marijuana available in a given year based on the amount seized during that year necessarily provides only a rough estimate. If only 10 percent of illicit drugs are seized in any given year, then, based on the figure of 2,412,365 pounds of marijuana seized in 2002, one could estimate that in 2002 the total amount of marijuana that traffickers succeeded in smuggling into the country was roughly 24 million pounds, or about 10,889 metric tons. If one doubles that amount to take into account the domestic production of marijuana that was not seized, then the total amount would be closer to 22,000 metric tons.

Indirect indicators related to seizures of illicit cannabis products also help to explain

| Table 9. Federal Marijuana Seizures, 1989-2002 | |
| (in pounds) | |
Year	Quantity Seized
2002	2,412,365
2001	2,674,826
2000	2,614,746
1999	2,282,313
1998	1,777,434
1997	1,488,362
1996	1,429,786
1995	1,308,171
1994	1,041,445
1993	772,086
1992	783,477
1991	499,097
1990	483,353
1989	1,070,965
Source: Based on information adapted by *Sourcebook* staff from tables provided by the U.S. Department of Justice, Drug Enforcement Administration, and Federal-wide Drug Seizure System, *Sourcebook of Criminal Justice Statistics Online*, Table 4.36.	

other aspects of the problem. For example, the origin of seized drugs helps to identify the main source countries for marijuana, and these include the United States itself. However, the origin of marijuana is difficult to determine unless it is seized at the grow site. Marijuana produced in and shipped from California is particularly difficult to distinguish from marijuana transshipped through California and produced in Mexico.[87] A large percentage of the marijuana seized in the United States is from foreign source areas.[88]

---

[86] U.S. DEA Public Affairs, "South Carolina," *Drug Trafficking in the United States*, July 25, 2003. [http://www.usdoj.gov/dea/pubs/state_factsheets.html]
[87] NDIC, *National Drug Threat Assessment 2001 - The Domestic Pers*pective, October 2000. [http://www.usdoj.gov/ndic/pubs/647/marijuan.htm#Top]
[88] United Nations Office on Drugs and Crime (UNODC), "Trafficking in Cannabis," Chapter 1.2.4, *Global Illicit Drug Trends, 2003* [Vienna, Austria], 72. [http://www.unodc.org/pdf/report_2003-06-26_1.pdf]

Most of the cannabis herb seizures in the world take place in the Americas. In 2001, the Americas accounted for 63 percent of all marijuana seizures worldwide. In that year, Mexico accounted for 39 percent of all marijuana seizures; and the United States, 15 percent. The

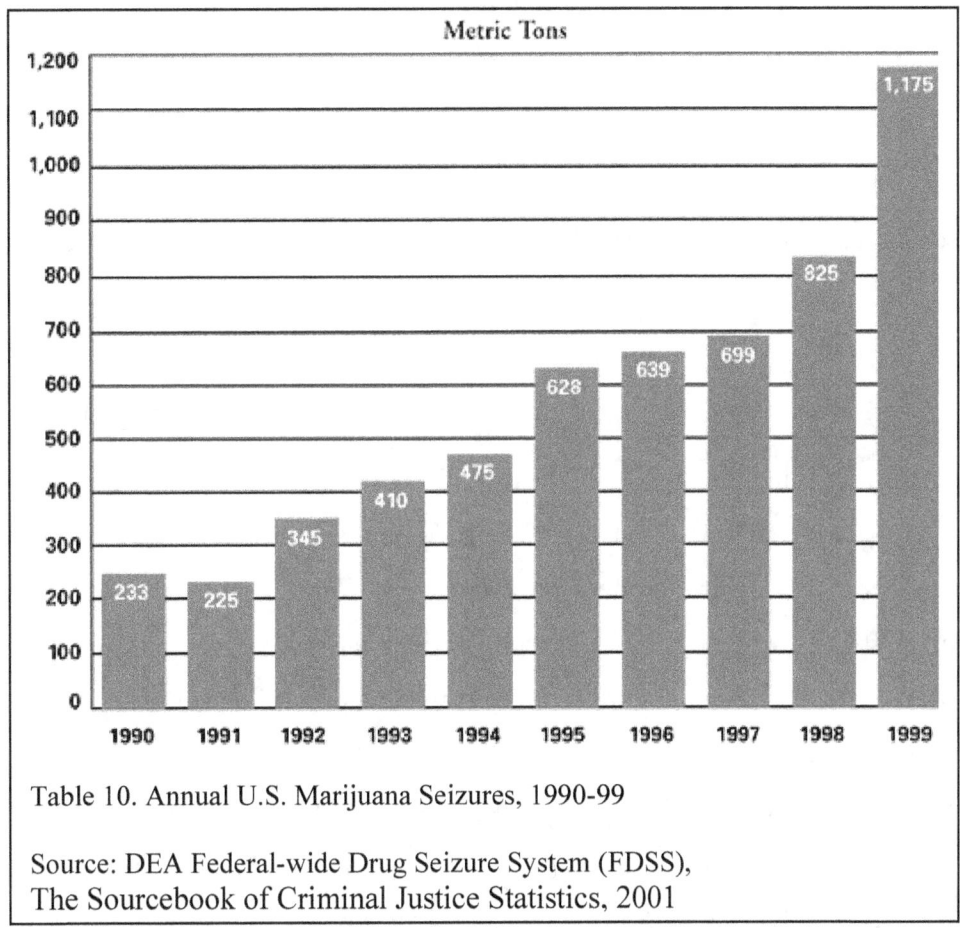

Table 10. Annual U.S. Marijuana Seizures, 1990-99

Source: DEA Federal-wide Drug Seizure System (FDSS),
The Sourcebook of Criminal Justice Statistics, 2001

combined total constituted 54 percent of the worldwide figure. While marijuana seizures have increased in North America since the 1990s, those of South America have declined since the mid-1990s.[89]

MAJOR AVENUES INTO THE UNITED STATES

There appear to be four principal avenues for smuggling marijuana into the continental United States: the Southwest border with Mexico, the Northwest and Northeast borders with Canada, and the Florida coastline (see Figure 2). These avenues allow marijuana to flow north from Mexico through the United States and to western and eastern Canada, northeast from the

---

[89] United Nations Office on Drugs and Crime (UNODC), "Trafficking in Cannabis," Chapter 1.2.4, *Global Illicit Drug Trends, 2003* (Vienna, Austria), 71. [http://www.unodc.org/pdf/report_2003-06-26_1.pdf]

Caribbean through Florida to the eastern United States and eastern Canada, and south from British Columbia in western Canada to the western and eastern United States. Elevated security since the September 11, 2001, terrorist attacks has deterred transportation of most drugs by commercial air travel, but smugglers are continuing to use parcel post and small aircraft.

From Canada

Traffickers transport drugs across the U.S.-Canada border at monitored and unmonitored points. These traffickers use a variety of methods, including smuggling by land, sea, air, and mail.[90]

By Land

Overland drug smuggling typically occurs along the Washington State-British Columbia border in the West, at the Detroit-Windsor and Buffalo points of entries in the Great Lakes area, and along the Quebec and Ontario borders with New York, Vermont, and Maine in the East. Mexican drug-trafficking organizations and criminal groups based in Mexico and California are the primary transporters of Mexico-produced marijuana and of marijuana produced by Mexican criminal groups in the western states.[91]

Along land borders, smugglers typically transport drugs by commercial, private, and rental vehicles; snowmobiles; and all-terrain vehicles. They also walk across the border carrying drugs in backpacks. Intelligence reports indicate that drug smugglers increasingly are using night-vision optics and Global Positioning System (GPS) equipment to navigate in remote areas. Drug shipments are secreted in duffel bags or luggage and in hidden compartments of commercial and private vehicles, or they are commingled with legitimate cargo in commercial vehicles crossing the border.

---

[90] NDIC, "Drug Threats - Drug Transportation Across the U.S.-Canada Border," United States-Canada Border Drug Threat Assessment, December 2001. [http://www.usdoj.gov/ndic/pubs07/794/transp.htm#Top]
[91] NDIC, Colorado *Drug Threat Assessment Update*, May 2003. [http://www.usdoj.gov/ndic/pubs4/4300/marijuan.htm#Top]

By Sea

Traffickers also transport drugs across the border using maritime smuggling methods. Drugs are commonly transported across marine borders in all types of pleasure craft, from cabin cruisers and sailing vessels to kayaks and personal watercraft. Maritime smuggling is most

prevalent in the Washington State-British Columbia area, where traffickers smuggle drugs by hiding shipments on vessels or having "mules" ride the regional ferry systems as drug-carrying passengers. The extent of maritime drug smuggling across the Great Lakes is largely unknown. Law enforcement and intelligence reports occasionally describe the smuggling of small amounts of drugs across the Great Lakes. To date, however, this type of information has been mostly anecdotal, and quantifying the maritime smuggling threat in the Great Lakes area has been difficult.

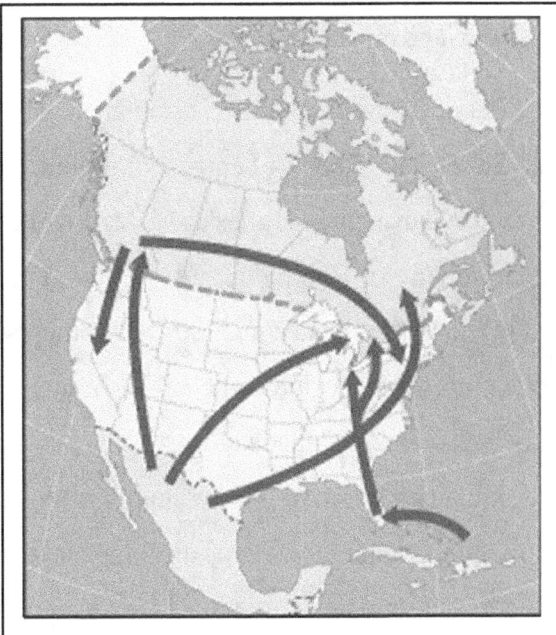

Figure 2. Cross-Border Marijuana Distribution in North America

Source: NDIC, December 2001.

By Air

Law enforcement reporting contains several examples of drug smuggling by aircraft from Canada to the United States. Drug smuggling by aircraft has occurred in a number of locations, including from British Columbia to Washington State, from the Vancouver area across the Idaho and Montana borders, across Lake Erie into Pennsylvania, and from Quebec to Maine. El Paso Intelligence Center (EPIC) reporting indicates continued suspicious small aircraft activity in Maine near Jackman, nine miles from the U.S.-Canada border, and at Rangely Airport, 21 miles from the border. Marijuana traffickers use small private aircraft to transport Canada-produced marijuana to the United States.

Traffickers increasingly are shipping illegal drugs across the U.S.-Canada border in mail parcels. Law enforcement reporting indicates that drugs (such as heroin, cocaine, and other dangerous drugs) and precursor chemicals are smuggled by mail and commercial parcel carriers because of the anonymity and efficiency of such delivery. Moreover, the RCMP reporting indicates that precursor chemicals purchased from legitimate chemical supply companies are shipped by mail to post office boxes registered under fictitious names.

From the Caribbean

Personal-use amounts of hashish are seized occasionally in the eastern and western United States and at ports of entry along the U.S.-Canada border. Large shipments of hashish destined for Canada sometimes are seized while in transit through the United States. One domestic seizure of 10.6 metric tons destined for Montreal accounted for nearly all of the hashish seized in the United States in 2000.[92] Shipments of hashish and liquid hashish flow from the Caribbean through Florida and New York then north to eastern Canada, and directly from the Caribbean to eastern Canada.

Jamaican criminal groups supply multi-metric ton quantities of marijuana to the United States.[93] Jamaican organizations also appear to be involved in dispatching Mexican marijuana by parcel carriers. Jamaican organized crime groups based in Ontario control most liquid hashish trafficking, smuggling primarily through airports. Traffickers transporting liquid hashish through the United States to Canada usually are linked to Canada-based criminal groups operating in southern Ontario and in the Atlantic Provinces.[94]

From Colombia

Colombia has been a major supplier of marijuana to the United States since at least the 1980s.[95] Large quantities of Colombian marijuana are smuggled by maritime vessels from South America to the United States via the Caribbean. Colombian marijuana is also transported from Colombia to Mexico by maritime vessel. Once in Mexico, marijuana typically is smuggled across the Southwest border into the United States.

---

[92] NDIC, "Marijuana Update," *Intelligence Brief: National Drug Threat Assessment*, Document ID: 2002-J0403-002, August 2002. [http://www.usdoj.gov/ndic/pubs1/1335/index.htm#Overview]
[93] NDIC, United States-Canada Border Drug Threat Assessment, December 2001.
[94]NDIC, U.S. Department of Justice, *United States-Canada Border Drug Threat Assessment*, December 2001.
[95] South America/Caribbean Strategic Intelligence Unit (NIBC) of the Office of International Intelligence, U.S. DEA Intelligence Division, *The Drug Trade in Colombia: A Threat Assessment* (DEA-02006), March 2002. [http://www.usdoj.gov/dea/pubs/intel/02006/index.html#6]

From Mexico

Mexican traffickers figure prominently in the distribution of drugs, including marijuana, in U.S. markets.[96] Organized crime groups operating from Mexico have smuggled marijuana into the United States since the early 1970s. These groups maintain extensive networks of associates, often related through familial or regional ties to associates living in the United States, where they control multi-drug smuggling and wholesale distribution from hub[97] cities to retail markets throughout the United States.[98] As Mexico's most widely produced drug, marijuana has the most routes and modes of transportation for being smuggled into the United States (see Figure 3).

Figure 3. Air, Land, and Sea Routes in Mexico Used by Mexican Drug Cartels to Smuggle Their Shipments into the United States.

Source: Report by Mexico's Office of the Attorney General, as cited by *El Norte* [Monterrey,

---

[96] Bureau for International Narcotics and Law Enforcement Affairs, U.S. Department of State, "Mexico," *International Narcotics Control Strategy Report, 2002*, March 2003. [http://www.state.gov/g/inl/rls/nrcrpt/2002/html/17944.htm]

[97] A transportation hub is defined as a city or area in the United States that is the destination of recurring shipments of wholesale quantities of drugs from a primary production area (foreign or domestic). Transportation hubs also function as distribution centers.

[98] U.S. DEA Public Affairs, *Drug Trafficking in the United States*, July 25, 2003.

Mexican authorities have determined, as a result of seizing a total of 515 tons of marijuana as of June 2003, that Mexican drug-trafficking organizations use seven federal highway routes, six air routes, and five maritime routes to smuggle marijuana into the United States.[99] Employing a variety of transportation and concealment methods to smuggle marijuana into the United States, drug-trafficking groups operating from Mexico move bulk shipments of marijuana north to the U.S. southwestern border area by land, sea, and air. They often break down the shipments to a more manageable and less detectable size at stash sites along the land border before smuggling them into the United States.

By Land

Transport across the border is primarily overland by commercial, private, and rental vehicles and by couriers on foot. Private aircraft and watercraft are used but to a lesser extent. Most shipments are smuggled into the United States through or between points of entry in Arizona, California, and Texas. FDSS data indicate that the 610,828 kilograms of marijuana seized by federal law enforcement officers in Texas in 2000 accounted for the great majority of the marijuana seized or purchased in DEA's System to Retrieve Information from Drug Evidence (STRIDE) for that year. [100]

Kansas is a transit state for Mexico-produced marijuana destined for drug markets throughout the United States. More than 80 percent of the 10,000 kilograms of marijuana seized on Kansas highways as part of Operation Pipeline in 2000 was destined for other areas, including Florida, Georgia, Illinois, Indiana, Iowa, Missouri, Ohio, Pennsylvania, and Washington, D.C.[101]

Although the list is not inclusive, cities most likely used as transportation hubs for marijuana smuggled from Mexico are Los Angeles and San Diego, California; Nogales and Phoenix, Arizona; and Brownsville, Dallas, El Paso, Houston, Laredo, McAllen, and San Antonio, Texas. These cities also function as distribution centers for marijuana shipped to

---

[99] *El Norte* [Monterrey, Mexico], October 14, 2003, as translated by FBIS LAP20031015000096, "Highlights: US-Mexico Border Crime, Narcotics, and Security Issues," October 14, 2003. [http://www.elnorte.com/ed_impresa/default.asp]

[100] NDIC, "Marijuana Update," *Intelligence Brief: National Drug Threat Assessment*, Document ID: 2002-J0403-002, August 2002; and NDIC, *Texas Drug Threat Assessment*, Document ID: 2003-S0387TX-001, October 2003. [http://www.usdoj.gov/ndic/pubs5/5624/index.htm]

[101] NDIC, "Marijuana Update," *Intelligence Brief: National Drug Threat Assessment*, Document ID: 2002-J0403-002, August 2002; and NDIC, *Texas Drug Threat Assessment*, Document ID: 2003-S0387TX-001, October 2003. [http://www.usdoj.gov/ndic/pubs5/5624/index.htm]

markets across the country.[102] The 2003 report by Mexico's Office of the Attorney General notes that the most drug-trafficking activity is seen in the Sonora-Arizona border area, which includes the Mexican cities of Agua Prieta, Nogales, and San Luis Río Colorado in Sonora State, where the groups headed by Joaquín "El Chapo" Guzmán and the heirs of Amado Carrillo Fuentes operation.[103]

The entire Southwest Border area is mainly a narcotics transshipment point. The EPIC (El Paso Intelligence Center) has documented that 65 percent of the narcotics that are sold in U.S. markets enter the country through the Southwest Border. The Southwest Border high-intensity drug-trafficking area is comprised of four distinct trafficking corridors called "plazas," which are used by the drug-trafficking organizations to ply their trade. The most transshipped narcotic in the area is marijuana.[104]

The EPIC drug seizure statistics reflect significant increases in marijuana seizures along the U.S. Southwest Border, the major transit area. Such seizures increased 56 percent from 1996 to 1998.[105] This trend of increasing seizures continued into the 1999-2002 period (see Table 11). Most of the New Mexico/Mexico international border (approximately 150 miles) is open desert and is generally uninhabited with innumerable roads, trails, footpaths, and ranches that allow smugglers easy entry into the United States and access to major highways that traverse the country.[106] West Texas, commonly referred to as the El Paso/Juárez Corridor, serves as the gateway for narcotics destined to major metropolitan areas in the United States.[107]

Sources-of-supply from Mexico move significant quantities of marijuana and cocaine through the points of entry using major east/west and north/south interstate highways that crisscross through the El Paso Division. These highways provide the traffickers with transportation routes for distribution of drugs throughout the country. Drug traffickers also obtain warehouses in El Paso for stash locations and recruit drivers from the area to transport the

---

[102] This paragraph derives from NDIC, "Marijuana Update," *Intelligence Brief: National Drug Threat Assessment*, Document ID: 2002-J0403-002, August 2002.
[103] *El Norte* [Monterrey, Mexico], October 14, 2003.
[104] White House, Office of National Drug Control Policy. "Southwest Border HIDTA," *High-Intensity Drug Trafficking Areas*, March 13, 2003. <http://www.whitehousedrugpolicy.gov/hidta/frames_sw.html>
[105] U.S. DEA, *Drug Intelligence Brief: The Cannabis Situation in the United States*, December 1999. [http://www.usdoj.gov/dea/pubs/intel/99028/99028.html] EPIC seizure statistics, such as those in Table 11, tend to be lower than FDSS statistics. For the latter, see the FDSS seizure statistics under the individual state sections in the Appendix.
[106] U.S. DEA, *Briefs and Background*, "New Mexico," http://www.usdoj.gov/dea/pubs/states/newmexico.html
[107] U.S. DEA, *Briefs and Background*, "New Mexico."

narcotics to various destinations throughout the United States. Additional threats to the region are the shipments of controlled substances by commercial vehicles, including aircraft, buses, and by Amtrak rail. El Paso is also considered a hub for significant amounts of drug proceeds being laundered through small businesses. The Southwest Border area of Texas is largely rural and sparsely populated and includes the Big Bend Corridor, a transshipment route for drugs entering the United States from Northeast Mexico en route to Midland/Odessa and other cities in the United States.[108]

Most of the marijuana smuggled into the United States from Mexico is concealed in vehicles—often in false compartments—or hidden in shipments of legitimate agricultural or industrial products. Marijuana also is smuggled across the border by rail, horse, raft, and backpack.[109] Shipments of 20 kilograms or less are smuggled by pedestrians who enter the United States at border

Table 11. Marijuana Seizures Within 150 Miles of the U.S.-Mexico Border, in Pounds, 1999-2002

	1999	2000	2001	2002
Arizona	169,586	197,036	212,229	246,161
California	191,569	230,110	202,046	126,161
New Mexico	35,079	45,209	51,527	37,347
Texas	402,567	459,619	592,771	604,993

Source: National Drug Intelligence Center (NDIC), *Texas Drug Threat Assessment*, Document ID: 2003-S0387TX-001, October 2003, citing El Paso Intelligence Center. [http://www.usdoj.gov/ndic/pubs5/5624/index.htm]

checkpoints and by backpackers who, alone or in groups ("mule trains"), cross the border at more remote locations.[110] Organized crime groups operating from Mexico conceal marijuana in an array of vehicles, including commercial vehicles, private automobiles, pickup trucks, vans, mobile homes, and horse trailers, driven through border ports of entry. Larger shipments ranging up to multi-thousand kilograms are usually smuggled in tractor-trailers. Marijuana packages are often wrapped in cellophane; coated with mustard, grease, and motor oil; and commingled in a load of other products, including anything from television sets to pickles.[111]

---

[108] U.S. DEA, *Briefs and Background*, "New Mexico," http://www.usdoj.gov/dea/pubs/states/newmexico.html
[109] U.S. DEA, *Drug Trafficking in the United States*, September 2001.
[110] U.S. DEA Public Affairs, *Drug Trafficking in the United States*, July 25, 2003.
[111] U.S. DEA Public Affairs, *Drug Trafficking in the United States*, July 25, 2003.

Another, more unconventional method of smuggling marijuana and other drugs into the United States from Mexico is cross-border tunneling. U.S. and Mexican officials discovered a one-year-old tunnel on April 4, 2003, that drug traffickers had built directly below a concrete tunnel used as a drainage pipe for rivers, rain, and water in general flowing between the two countries.[112] U.S. authorities discovered another tunnel, which was used "to introduce marijuana and cocaine into U.S. territory," according to Mexican prosecutors, on September 12, 2003, in Tijuana. Measuring 492 feet long, five feet high, and 2½ feet wide, it runs from Mexicali in Baja California, Mexico, to Calexico, California.[113] Five such constructions have been discovered in the border area so far in 2003. In 2002, U.S. drug agents discovered a

Entrance to Drug-Smuggling Tunnel Discovered in Tijuana, Mexico, on April 4, 2003

Source: *Frontera* [Tijuana, Mexico], April 9, 2003.

1,200-foot tunnel—complete with electric lights, ventilation ducts, and wooden walls—in a remote section of rocky border scrubland, 70 miles east of San Diego near a small town called Tecate. Investigators believe that the notorious Tijuana Cartel, headed by several brothers in the Arellano Félix family, built the tunnel at least two or three years earlier.[114]

---

[112] Agustín Pérez Aguilar, "Resulta difícil destruir tunnel" [It Will Be Difficult to Destroy Tunnel], *Frontera* [Tijuana, Mexico], April 9, 2003.
[http://www.frontera.info/EdicionImpresa/ejemplaresanteriores/BusquedaEjemplares.asp?numnota=191377&fecha=09/04/2003]
[113] ACAN/EFE Press Agency [Panama City], September 17, 2003.
[114] Kevin Sullivan, "Billions in Drugs Moved Via Tunnel: Lucrative Drug-Smuggling Mechanism Discovered," *Washington Post*, March 2, 2002.

By Sea

Besides engaging in overland smuggling, drug traffickers use ocean vessels to move Mexican marijuana up the coast of Mexico to U.S. ports, drop-off sites along the U.S. coast, or to rendezvous points with other boats bound for the United States. Law enforcement authorities in southern California indicate that marijuana is transferred from mother ships in international waters to Mexican fishing vessels. The smaller vessels then deliver the marijuana to overland smugglers on the Mexican Baja California Peninsula. From there, the marijuana is generally moved to border transit points and then carried to the Los Angeles metropolitan area for distribution to eastern markets.[115] The 2003 report by Mexico's Office of the Attorney General notes that currently the Sea of Cortez is most often used to transport drugs by water.[116]

By Air

Other smuggling methods have included parcel post. In April 2000, U.S. anti-narcotics agents broke up a drug ring that used corrupt employees of the parcel service Federal Express (FedEx) to transport marijuana around the country. The DEA arrested more than 100 people, including 25 FedEx employees, who provided company aircraft and trucks to

The Tecate tunnel was discovered in 2002.
Source: DEA, July 2002

distribute US$160 million worth of marijuana. Organized by a powerful Mexican drug gang, the operation smuggled bales of marijuana to Jamaican traffickers in California, who then used FedEx to deliver them to dealers across the United States.[117]

---

[115] U.S. DEA Public Affairs, *Drug Trafficking in the United States*, July 25, 2003.
[116] *El Norte* [Monterrey, Mexico], October 14, 2003.
[117] BBC News Online, "US Busts Drug Express," April 14, 2000.
[http://news.bbc.co.uk/1/hi/world/americas/712831.stm]

LINKS TO ORGANIZED CRIME

Major Trafficking Organizations

The demographic makeup of marijuana producers in the United States includes a wide range of racial, ethnic, and social groups and often reflects the general population of an area. Law enforcement reporting indicates that most local, usually independent, growers are Caucasian, although across the United States local growers also are identified as Mexican, Hispanic, and African American. Those identified in more regional or localized areas include Jamaicans (New England, New York/New Jersey, and Mid-Atlantic regions as well as Florida), Vietnamese and Asians (Pacific Northwest), Native Americans (Montana, New Mexico, New York, South Dakota, and Wisconsin), Colombians (Florida), and Dominicans (Rhode Island). Organized groups involved in cultivation and production include outlaw motorcycle gangs and drug-trafficking organizations.[118]

Canada

During the 1996-2001 period, criminal groups based in Canada emerged as suppliers of high-grade marijuana to the United States. Organized criminal groups such as outlaw motorcycle gangs transport shipments of Canada-produced marijuana to U.S. markets; the wide-ranging involvement of such gangs in the marijuana trade is well documented in law enforcement and intelligence reporting. Outlaw motorcycle gangs such as the Hells Angels, however, are now faced with fierce competition from Vietnamese criminal groups in western Canada. Vietnamese gangs have been steadily encroaching on the lucrative marijuana-growing industry historically controlled by outlaw bike gangs in Ontario and British Columbia.[119] Canadian police data indicate that Vietnamese gang activity in Vancouver's cannabis cultivation industry increased almost 20-fold between 1997 and 2000.[120] Asian organized crime groups are entrenched in British Columbia, Alberta, and Ontario and are expanding marijuana cultivation in

---

[118] This paragraph derives from NDIC, "Marijuana Update," *Intelligence Brief: National Drug Threat Assessment*, Document ID: 2002-J0403-002, August 2002. [http://www.usdoj.gov/ndic/pubs1/1335/index.htm#Overview]
[119] This paragraph is based on Peter O'Neil, CanWest News Service, "Canada a 'Haven' for Marijuana Growers; RCMP Fears Gang Involvement, 'Extreme Violence,'" Canada.com [Toronto; Internet www-text], May 9, 2003.
[120] NDIC, *United States-Canada Border Drug Threat Assessment*, December 2001.
[http://www.usdoj.gov/ndic/pubs07/794/marijuan.htm#Map%201]

Saskatchewan, Manitoba, Quebec, and Atlantic Canada.[121] These operations are typically highly organized with extensive interprovincial networks and drug-distribution networks to the United States.

The bulk of the marijuana grown in British Columbia is exported to the United States, where there is a large market and a higher profit margin. Marijuana produced in lower British Columbia may be transported to Ontario by rail and then into the United States in tractor-trailer trucks. It is estimated that, in the city of Vancouver alone, there are approximately 10,000 clandestine marijuana grow operations. Profits generated by Vietnamese-based criminal groups through the cultivation and trafficking of marijuana are often reinvested to finance other illicit activities, or laundered money is invested into legitimate businesses. These Asian organized crime groups associate with other organized crime groups nationally and internationally, particularly in the United States and Southeast Asia.[122]

British Columbia's highly potent marijuana (BC Bud) is sometimes exchanged in the United States for harder drugs such as cocaine and hard-to-get handguns. For example, three men were arrested in British Columbia in February 2003 after sneaking across the Canada-U.S. border with dozens of guns, diamonds, and U.S. cash. Police believed that they were likely involved in an organized crime guns-for-drugs deal.[123]

Mexico

According to Mexico's Office of the Attorney General's, Mexico's seven major cartels are: the Arellano Félix in Tijuana, the Armando Valencia or Millennium, the Osiel Cárdenas-Guillén on the Gulf Coast, the Amezcua in Colima, the Joaquín "El Chapo" Guzmán in Sinaloa, the Diáz Parada in Oaxaca, and the Vicente Carrillo-Fuentes in Juárez. Another prominent major Mexican drug-trafficking group involved in trafficking in marijuana in the United States is the Miguel Caro-Quintero. As of September 2003, the border-based Vicente Carrillo-Fuentes or Juárez Cartel had become Mexico's most powerful drug-trafficking organization, operating in 17

---

[121] This paragraph is based on Criminal Intelligence Service Canada (CISC), "Asian-Based Organized Crime," *Annual Report on Organized Crime in Canada 2003*, 19-20.
[http://www.cisc.gc.ca/AnnualReport2003/Document/CISC%202003%20Annual%20Report.pdf]
[122] This paragraph is based on Criminal Intelligence Service Canada (CISC), "Asian-Based Organized Crime," *Annual Report on Organized Crime in Canada 2003*, 19-20.
[123] *The Globe and Mail* [Toronto; Internet version-www], February 20, 2003.

of the 32 states in the country.[124] These organizations are responsible for the majority of the marijuana entering the United States.[125]

In addition to the aforementioned major marijuana trafficking groups, recent and historical intelligence has identified the Durango-based Herrera family as one of the larger Mexican drug-trafficking organizations. However, its trafficking in marijuana is a relatively minor part of its business, in comparison with its heroin and cocaine trafficking.[126]

Arellano-Félix

During the period from the mid-1980s to 2002, the Arellano-Félix was one of the most powerful and violent drug-trafficking organizations in Mexico. From strongholds in Tijuana and Mexicali, the Arellano-Félix orchestrates the transportation, importation, and distribution of multi-ton quantities of marijuana and other drugs into the United States. However, the Arellano-Félix was dealt two huge blows in February and March 2002— the death of its notorious and

Benjamín Arellano-Félix   Ramón Arellano-Félix

brutal enforcer, Ramón Arellano-Félix, on February 10, 2002, and the arrest of its overall chief of operations, Benjamín Arellano-Félix, on March 9, 2002.[127] The Arellano-Félix operated primarily in Tijuana, and between San Diego and Los Angeles in the United States. The two setbacks suffered by the Arellano-Félix in early 2002 may have weakened its ability to retain control over the Tijuana drug-trafficking corridor. Although the Arellano-Félix reportedly has developed ties to Russian organized crime and to the Revolutionary Armed Forces of Colombia (Fuerzas Armadas Revolucionarias de Colombia—FARC), which is a guerrilla and terrorist organization, the Arellano-Félix-FARC relationship appears to be based on cocaine and not marijuana.

---

[124] Mónica Medel, "Mexico's Juárez Cartel Said Most Powerful Drug Trafficking Organization," ACANEFE [Panama City], September 4, 2003, citing the Mexican Office of the Attorney General.
[125] "Mexico Country Brief," *Drug Intelligence Brief*, July 2002, U.S. DEA.
[http://www.dea.gov/pubs/intel/02035/02035.html]
[126] U.S. DEA "The Mexican Heroin Trade," April 2000 (DEA-20014).
<http://www.usdoj.gov/dea/pubs/intel/20014/20014.html>
[127] *Reforma* [Mexico City; Internet version-www], March 10, 2002, as translated by FBIS LAP20020312000111, "Arellano Felix Family Business, a History."

Vicente Carrillo-Fuentes

Although the core business of the Carrillo-Fuentes or Juárez Cartel is smuggling Colombian cocaine into the United States, the group also deals in marijuana and other drugs. Since the death of former kingpin Amado Carrillo-Fuentes in July 1997, the structure of the Carrillo-Fuentes drug-trafficking organization has remained mostly intact with key lieutenants retaining control of specific geographic areas. These lieutenants include Amado's brother, Vicente Carrillo-Fuentes, Juan José Esparragosa-Moreno, and Ismael ("El Mayo") Zambada-García. Vicente Carrillo-Fuentes is wanted in Mexico and the United States in connection with a 46-count indictment that includes charges of importing and distributing thousands of kilograms of marijuana.[128] However, after the death of Amado Carrillo Fuentes, the Juárez Cartel shifted to a command structure based on a board of directors that, in addition to the aforementioned names, includes Beltrán Leyva and Ignácio Coronel.[129]

Armando Valencia-Cornelio

Armando Valencia-Cornelio, a Mexican national, is another significant drug trafficker operating in Mexico, and is a key figure in the interrelationship between major Mexican and Colombian drug-trafficking organizations. The Valencia-Cornelio group's primary bases of operation are in Guadalajara, Jalisco State; and the state of Michoacán.

Armando Valencia-Cornelio

Miguel Caro-Quintero

The Caro-Quintero organization, based in Sonora State, focuses on trafficking in cocaine and marijuana. Originally headed by Rafael Caro-Quintero, Miguel Angel Caro-Quintero became the head of the organization after the 1985 imprisonment of his brother, Rafael, on drug violations and his involvement in the murder of DEA Special Agent Enrique Camarena. Although Miguel was arrested in 1992, that effort was nullified when a Mexican federal judge in Hermosillo, Sonora, dropped all criminal charges and ordered his release from custody. Until his re-arrest on December 20, 2001, Miguel Caro-Quintero operated freely throughout northwestern

---

[128] FBI Wanted Fugitives, September 2002. <http://www.fbi.gov/mostwant/fugitive/sept2002/septfuentes.htm>
[129] Mónica Medel, "Mexico's Juárez Cartel Said Most Powerful Drug Trafficking Organization," ACANEFE [Panama City], September 4, 2003.

Mexico, running his drug-smuggling activities from Caborca, Sonora. Miguel Caro-Quintero is also known to have strong ties in Hermosillo.

Osiel Cárdenas-Guillén

The Cárdenas Guillén organization, formerly known as the Gulf Cartel, together with the Arellano Félix and Carillo Fuentes organizations, has been one of the three enduring pillars of

Osiel Cárdenas Guillén under arrest, March 13, 2003

Source: DEA

Mexican polydrug trafficking. Osiel Cárdenas-Guillén, a marijuana and cocaine trafficker responsible for the November 9, 1999, attempted assault and abduction of a DEA agent and a FBI agent in Matamoros, Tamaulipas State, is considered a leader of the remnants of the Gulf Cartel. Mexican authorities captured Cárdenas-Guillén, one of the most wanted, feared, and violent drug traffickers in the world, on March 14, 2003.

LINKS TO TERRORISM

Open-source reporting on possible connections between terrorist groups and marijuana trafficking in the United States has been very limited. The involvement of the indigenous Colombian guerrilla/terrorist groups, particularly the FARC and, to a lesser extent, the National Liberation Army (Ejército Nacional de Liberación—ELN), in the cocaine trade is well known. There have been numerous reports of FARC and ELN members being captured with marijuana shipments in Colombia or simply extorting protection money from marijuana cultivators. However, whether these groups are actively involved in smuggling marijuana into the United States is unclear.

There are indications of possible terrorist connections to marijuana smuggling from Canada and Mexico into the United States and marijuana cultivation in the United States itself. These apparent connections have yet to be well documented, but they may prove to be more substantial as more information becomes available.

With regard to Canada, if there is any terrorist connection to Canadian marijuana smuggling to the United States, the major news media apparently have not reported on it in recent years. However, there appears to be a strong potential for such a link to develop, if it does not already exist. As many as 50 international terrorist groups have a presence in Canada, and a few of them may see the fund-raising potential in the lucrative marijuana trade. For example, a May 2003 report by the Canadian Security Intelligence Service (CSIS) has warned police that members of the Palestinian Islamic Jihad (PIJ) terrorist group—supported by Iran and Syria with funding, training, and sanctuary—may try to infiltrate Canada to set up a support base in Canada similar to their fund-raising network in Florida. In February 2003, the *National Post* reported that Islamic Jihad had tried to obtain a fraudulent visa so that its treasurer, Muhammed Tasir Hassan Al-Khatib, could come to Canada.[130]

Some unspecified terrorist groups in Central Asia may have a role in smuggling hashish through Maine or possibly Massachusetts to Canada. The RCMP (Royal Canadian Mounted Police) has indicated that Afghan and Pakistani terrorist groups are financed by approximately US$20 million of illicit funds derived from the sale of hashish in Canada.[131] The increasing popularity of hashish in Canada is expected to change the hashish situation in Maine. Traffickers have moved hashish and hash oil through Maine and into Canada. It would appear, therefore, that Afghan and Pakistani terrorist groups may also have a role in the trafficking of hashish to a select few locations in the United States, such as Maine and possibly Boston, Massachusetts.

One of the few U.S. newspapers to report on a possible Hizballah connection with the marijuana trade in the United States is the *Los Angeles Times*, which, in May 2003, published a particularly informative article in this regard in its back pages.[132] The paper reported that marijuana cultivation in California's Sequoia National Park has increased steadily since the early 1990s, and that the number of plants seized in the state's oldest national park has jumped eightfold since 2001. Although most of Sequoia's cannabis cultivation is hidden in the steep Sierra Nevada foothills in the remote southwestern reaches of the park, large plots have been discovered a dozen miles from park headquarters. According to U.S. drug enforcement officials cited by the *Los Angeles Times*, the cannabis fields are financed by the Mexican drug cartels that dominate the methamphetamine trade in the adjacent Central Valley. The officials say there is evidence that the cartels, in turn, have financial ties to Middle Eastern smugglers linked to

---

[130] This paragraph is based on Stewart Bell, "Islamic Jihad coming to Canada, CSIS fears; Terrorists in U.S.: report," *National Post* [Internet Version-www], October 22, 2003.

[131] U.S. DEA, *Drug Intelligence Brief: Money Laundering in Canada,* August 2003, citing The Associated Press, July 14, 2002. [http://www.usdoj.gov/dea/pubs/intel/03034/03034.html#6]

[132] This discussion is based on Julie Cart, "Park's Pot Problem Explodes; Number of Marijuana Plants Seized at Sequoia Has Soared; Officials Say Mexican Cartels Linked to Mideast Terrorists Run the Operation," *Los Angeles Times*, May 14, 2003: B1

Hizballah and other terrorist groups. Ron Gravitt, special agent in charge at the Sacramento headquarters of California's Bureau of Narcotics Enforcement told the *Los Angeles Times*:

> Our belief is that the Mexican drug organizations have gone heavily into marijuana operations. The overhead is much lower than running a methamphetamine lab. They are taking the money from meth and putting it into expanding marijuana growing.

Furthermore, officials at the state narcotics agency and the DEA have pointed out that the Mexican cartels appear—on the basis on statements from informants and wiretaps—to have financial ties to Middle Eastern groups.[133] Bill Ruzzamenti, director of the state's High Intensity Drug Trafficking Area (HIDTA) program for the Central Valley and a former DEA agent, was quoted: "We have a number of methamphetamine cases where we've made a direct connection between the Hizballah and Mexican cartels." According to the *Los Angeles Times*, the DEA suspects that associates of the Lebanon-based Hizballah have been smuggling large amounts of pseudoephedrine tablets—pseudoephedrine is a key ingredient of methamphetamine— in cars and trucks across the Canadian border for sale to the drug cartels in California. The state narcotics bureau suspect that the cartels are using profits from the resale of the pseudoephedrine to bankroll the sharp increase in marijuana cultivation on public land.

Both al-Qa'ida and Hizballah have been reported to have members based in Canada and Mexico. There has been some speculation since 2001 that Islamic terrorist organizations, including the Sunni Muslim al Qa'ida network and the Lebanese Shi'ite Hizballah organization, have sought to establish a presence in that country, and that Hizballah may have established cells in northern Mexico, such as in Monterrey, which has sizable ethnic Lebanese and Palestinian communities.[134]

OUTLOOK

In the assessment of the NDIC, marijuana will remain the most widely available illicit drug in the United States. Domestic cannabis cultivation is likely to increase, while traffickers in foreign source countries will continue to smuggle marijuana into the United States to profit from high demand. The market for marijuana will remain strong given the drug's wide appeal and

---

[133] This paragraph is based on Cart, "Park's Pot Problem Explodes."

[134] For further details, see Ramón Miró, *Organized Crime and Terrorist Activity in Mexico, 1999-2002*, Library of Congress, Federal Research Division, February 2003: 43-44 [http://www.loc.gov/rr/frd/terrorism.html].

profit potential.[135] Most national data since the late 1990s indicate continuing overall stability in marijuana use. However, some national substance abuse indicators, including increased use and production of high-potency marijuana, suggest that demand may increase, according to the NDIC.[136]

Organized crime groups are likely to continue becoming increasingly involved in cannabis cultivation in the United States as well as in the transportation and distribution of marijuana throughout the country.[137] Mexican organizations will continue to dominate wholesale marijuana distribution for the near future. But several state and local agencies express concern that given the increasing demand for marijuana and what appears to be increasing tacit approval of marijuana use, the profit potential will attract individuals and criminal groups not currently involved in cannabis cultivation and marijuana distribution.[138]

The Criminal Intelligence Service Canada (CISC) believes that Asian organized crime will expand its involvement in the growing and exporting of marijuana in order to take advantage of high profits, low risks, and relatively lenient sentences.[139] In the assessment of the NDIC, marijuana smuggling from Canada to the United States probably will increase if the U.S. domestic demand for high-grade marijuana continues. Canadian marijuana production, largely controlled by Asian criminal groups and the Hells Angels organized motorcycle gang, will spread to previously unaffected areas of Canada through the established networks of these criminal groups, thereby facilitating increased marijuana smuggling to the United States. However, compared with the large quantities of marijuana smuggled across the U.S.-Mexico border, the threat that marijuana smuggling from Canada poses to the United States will remain low.[140]

---

[135] NDIC, *National Drug Threat Assessment 2002*, December 2001.
[http://www.usdoj.gov/ndic/pubs07/716/marijuan.htm#Top]
[136] NDIC, *National Drug Threat Assessment 2001 - The Domestic Per*spective, October 2000.
[http://www.usdoj.gov/ndic/pubs/647/marijuan.htm#Top]; and NDIC, *National Drug Threat Assessment 2003*, January 2003.
[137] NDIC, *National Drug Threat Assessment 2003*, January 2003.
[138] NDIC, *National Drug Threat Assessment 2001 - The Domestic Per*spective, October 2000.
[http://www.usdoj.gov/ndic/pubs/647/marijuan.htm#Top]
[139] Criminal Intelligence Service Canada (CISC), "Asian-Based Organized Crime," *Annual Report on Organized Crime in Canada 2003*, 19-21.
[http://www.cisc.gc.ca/AnnualReport2003/Document/CISC%202003%20Annual%20Report.pdf]
[140] NDIC, *United States-Canada Border Drug Threat Assessment*, December 2001.

APPENDIX: CANNABIS HERB DATA FOR U.S. STATES AND ASSOCIATED U.S. TERRITORIES[141]

I. U.S. STATES

ALABAMA

Marijuana Situation: Marijuana has long had a strong presence in Alabama. However, in the past few years, a transformation has been seen in the level of dealers in the area and in the size of loads commonly seized, especially in the Huntsville area. Only a few years ago, a seizure of 10 pounds of marijuana was fairly rare and considered significant, but now Huntsville authorities commonly seize loads of 50 to 100 pounds.

Production: The overall production of marijuana within the state continues to decline.

Indoor Domestic Grows: No information available.

Outdoor Domestic Grows: No information available.

Processed and Imported: Marijuana imported from Mexico is most common.

Federal Drug (Marijuana) Seizures, 2002: 819.5 kilograms

Major Avenues into the State: The main source of marijuana coming into the state is Mexico, with connections to South America as well as through port cities of Florida and the port of Mobile. African-American and Mexican criminal groups transport multi-kilogram to multi-hundred kilogram shipments of marijuana to Alabama from the Southwest Border. Marijuana is typically transported into the state by commercial and private vehicles, and by package delivery and express mail services. The transportation of marijuana into the state by the highway system is increasing. Even though the highway system is a confirmed route for most of the marijuana seized in the state, the international airports in the state could be another strong possibility.

Links to Organized Crime: African-American and Mexican criminal groups.

ALASKA

Marijuana Situation: Marijuana is the most abused and widespread illegal drug in Alaska.

Production: Most domestically produced marijuana is grown indoors.

---

[141] Unless noted otherwise, the data in this section come from U.S. DEA Public Affairs, *Drug Trafficking in the United States*, July 25, 2003. [http://www.usdoj.gov/dea/pubs/state_factsheets.html]

Indoor Domestic Grows: About 95 percent of Alaska's production of marijuana is grown indoors.

Outdoor Domestic Grows: Less than 5 percent of the marijuana in Alaska is grown outdoors.

Processed and Imported: No information available.

Federal Drug (Marijuana) Seizures, 2002: 0.9 kilograms.

Links to Organized Crime: No information available.

ARIZONA

Marijuana Situation: Arizona is directly north of the Mexican State of Sonora, a major trafficker stronghold. Arizona serves primarily as a drug importation and transshipment state.

Production:

Indoor Domestic Grows: No information available.

Outdoor Domestic Grows: No information available.

Processed and Imported: Marijuana imported from Mexico is common.

Federal Drug (Marijuana) Seizures, 2002: 24,965.1 kilograms.

Earlier Federal Drug Marijuana Seizures: Marijuana seizures in 2001 were 468,231 pounds. This figure represents a 22 percent drop from 2000 (see Table 12).[142]

Major Avenues into the State: Along the 350 miles of Arizona's border with Mexico border are three principal ports of entry (Nogales, Douglas, and San Luis) and three secondary ports of entry (Lukeville, Sasabe, and Naco). Most of the border area consists of inhospitable desert and steep mountain ranges, which are sparsely populated, infrequently patrolled by law enforcement, and ideal for drug smuggling. Multi-hundred kilogram quantities of marijuana are transported from Mexico to the United States throughout the Ports of Entry along the Southern Arizona

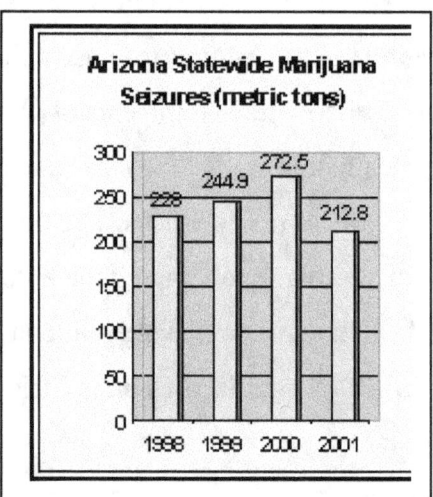

Table 12. Arizona Statewide Marijuana Seizures, 1998-2001

Source: Office of National Drug Control Policy

---

[142] Office of National Drug Control Policy, Southwest Border HIDTA Arizona Partnership, "Arizona: Threat Abstract," *Southwest Border: High-Intensity Drug Trafficking Areas*, March 13, 2003. [http://www.whitehousedrugpolicy.gov/hidta/frames_az.html]

border. In fenced areas along the border, bundles of marijuana are passed through holes, which have been cut, or the bundles of marijuana are simply thrown over the fence. Mexican trafficking groups use tractor-trailers, passenger vehicles, animal caravans and backpackers to smuggle the marijuana in quantities of between 25 and 300 kilograms.

Links to Organized Crime: Major Mexican trafficking organizations dominate drug smuggling and transportation. These groups are polydrug-trafficking organizations whose smuggling includes marijuana. A total of 410 drug-trafficking organizations were identified in CY 2001, and more than 50 percent of them have international connections.

ARKANSAS[143]

Marijuana Situation: Marijuana is the most widely available and frequently abused illicit drug in Arkansas. Seizure data reflect the ready availability of marijuana in Arkansas (see Table 13). Most of the marijuana available in the state is produced in Mexico. Mexican criminal groups and local independent dealers are the primary wholesale- and retail-level marijuana distributors in the state. Marijuana typically is distributed at the retail level from bars, strip clubs, schools, parking lots, residences, businesses, and at concerts. Arkansas is a transit state for marijuana shipments destined for drug markets throughout the United States. Marijuana transported via I-30 and I-40 through Arkansas, primarily from California and Texas, generally is destined for states in the Midwest and along the East Coast. Some cannabis is cultivated locally and distributed to other states, including Mississippi and Texas.

Production: Most of the marijuana available in Arkansas is produced in Mexico; however, some cannabis is cultivated throughout the state, primarily by local independent Caucasian growers.

Indoor Domestic Grows: Law enforcement officers have encountered indoor cultivation sites throughout Arkansas.

Outdoor Domestic Grows: In most areas of the state, cannabis is cultivated at outdoor grow sites. In Arkansas outdoor cannabis cultivation sites typically yield more cannabis per site than indoor sites.

Processed and Imported: Marijuana produced in Mexico, particularly commercial-grade marijuana, is the most widely available type of the drug in the state.

---

[143] This section also incorporates data from the NDIC, "Marijuana," *Arkansas Drug Threat Assessment*, October 2003. [http://www.usdoj.gov/ndic/pubs6/6184/marijuan.htm#Top]

Federal Drug (Marijuana) Seizures, 2002: 401.2 kilograms (DEA figure).

Table 13. Annual Amounts of Marijuana Seized in Arkansas, 1998-2002 (in kilograms)		
Year	Amount Seized (FDSS data)	Amount Seized (Operation Pipeline)*
1998	1,149.6	
1999	1,273.2	
2000	1,856.6	4,327
2001	2,281.1	1,325
2002	1,330.1	

Source: National Drug Intelligence Center, "Marijuana," Arkansas Drug Threat Assessment, October 2003, citing Federal-wide Drug Seizure System (FDSS) data.
* EPIC 2001 Operation Pipeline data

Major Avenues into the State: Marijuana typically is transported into Arkansas in hidden compartments in private and commercial vehicles, and occasionally by couriers on buses, via the same routes used to transport methamphetamine and cocaine. Transporters use a variety of means to conceal marijuana during transportation, including boxes, metal containers, duffel bags, suitcases, and compartments installed in the side panels, floors, and tailgates of vehicles. Transporters also intermingle marijuana with legitimate items such as produce or conceal the drugs in luggage. Marijuana typically is wrapped in layers of cellophane and duct tape and covered with mustard or coffee grounds to mask the odor of the drug. The majority of marijuana arrests and seizures in Arkansas are from Operation Pipeline stops, as the vehicles transit through the state, and from parcel interceptions. Seizures in excess of 1,000 pounds are typically concealed in tractor-trailers destined for cities on the East Coast.

Links to Organized Crime: Mexican organized crime groups are the primary transporters of wholesale quantities of Mexico-produced marijuana into and through Arkansas. Local independent dealers, primarily Caucasians, and street gangs also transport marijuana into the state. These transporters generally smuggle the drug into Arkansas from Mexico, California, and southwestern states.

CALIFORNIA

Marijuana Situation: Marijuana is the most widely available and abused illicit drug in California. Drugs such as marijuana are smuggled into the state from Mexico; however, marijuana is also produced or cultivated in large quantities within the state. Marijuana, both domestic and imported (from Mexico), is widely available in San Diego and Imperial Counties. It also continues to be the drug of choice (with methamphetamine) in the San Diego and Imperial County area. There is an increase in narcotics trafficking in the eastern section of San Diego, as well as in Imperial County.

Authorities in Southern California have seized more marijuana than all other drugs combined. Marijuana also has shown the biggest increase in the number of users, particularly among those 18 and younger. Mexican marijuana predominates in the region, but marijuana from Canada (BC Bud) and domestically produced marijuana are also available. The primary wholesalers are Mexican drug-trafficking organizations who use middlemen to move the marijuana to street-level dealers. Mexican drug-trafficking organizations smuggle large amounts of marijuana into and through the district, using it as both a destination and a transshipment point.[144]

Production: Domestically produced marijuana is preferred in California because of the higher THC (tetrahydrocannabinol) content. California-grown marijuana usually contains 10 to 20 percent THC, versus 2 to 5 percent for the Mexican variety.[145]

Indoor Domestic Grows: Potent domestic marijuana is cultivated in sophisticated indoor, hydroponic gardens throughout the state. Statewide, cultivation has increased since California's voters passed Proposition 215, the Compassionate Use Act of 1996, removing state legal sanctions for marijuana used to alleviate specific medical conditions with a doctor's recommendation. Cannabis "clubs" or "cooperatives" have established themselves as illegal distributors under the guise of "caregivers."

Outdoor Domestic Grows: The cultivation of cannabis is widespread in Northern California, especially in the Emerald Triangle (Mendocino, Trinity and Humboldt counties). The large-scale outdoor cultivation sites that dot the Emerald Triangle often use sophisticated irrigation systems to produce thousands of pounds of high-grade, high-demand marijuana annually. Cannabis cultivators in this area are predominantly young Caucasian males.[146]

---

[144] This paragraph is based on NDIC, *California Southern District Drug Threat Assessment,* Document ID: 2001-S0387SCA-001, May 2002. [http://www.usdoj.gov/ndic/pubs/654/index.htm#Contents]

[145] NDIC, *California Northern and Eastern Districts Drug Threat Assessment*, January 2001. [http://www.usdoj.gov/ndic/pubs/653/marijuan.htm#Top]

[146] NDIC, *California Northern and Eastern Districts Drug Threat Assessment*, January 2001.

Growers increasingly use state and federal lands to cultivate cannabis. The U.S. Forest Service reports that seizures in the Cleveland, San Bernardino, and Angeles National Forests increased over 300 percent in the 1999-2001 period. The Forest Service seized 49,126 pounds of cannabis in 1997 and 237,329 pounds in 1999 in the three areas.[147] Mexican drug-trafficking organizations run large-scale cannabis operations in the national forests of the Central District (counties of Los Angeles, Orange, Riverside, San Bernardino, San Luis Obispo, Santa Barbara, and Ventura) sending crews from Mexico to tend cannabis crops. They also hire illegal immigrants to manage and watch over the cannabis cultivation sites. The growers make camp near the plots and live onsite until harvest is completed. Cultivating cannabis in remote areas of national forests reduces the risks and costs associated with smuggling marijuana across the Southwest Border. The use of public lands to cultivate cannabis is appealing to domestic growers because the risk of asset forfeiture is substantially minimized.[148]

Processed and Imported: Most of the marijuana available in the state is produced in Mexico, but cannabis is also cultivated throughout the state.

Federal Drug (Marijuana) Seizures, 2002: 11,172.7 kilograms.

Earlier Federal Drug (Marijuana) Seizures: During 2001, California Border Alliance Group (CBAG) task forces and participating member agencies seized more than 209,675 kilograms of marijuana.[149] The rate of marijuana seizures in California over the 1995-99 period shows a 238 percent change. In 1995, 56,737 pounds were seized; in 1996, 169,287; in 1997, 138,662; in 1998, 186,941; and in 1999, 191,514 (see Table 14).

Major Avenues into the State: Large quantities of low-grade marijuana are transported overland through Mexico to the California-Mexico border. Highly potent Canadian marijuana (BC Bud) is also transported into the state. San Diego remains a principal transshipment zone for a variety of drugs, particularly marijuana, smuggled from Mexico. However, traffickers are looking for alternate routes to smuggle narcotics into the country because of the more thorough screening of people and vehicles entering the United States from Mexico at San Ysidro, California. Calexico's West Port of Entry, located in downtown Calexico, California,

---

[147] This paragraph is based on NDIC, *California Southern District Drug Threat Assessment*, May 2002.
[148] NDIC, *California Central District Drug Threat Assessment*, May 2001.
[http://www.usdoj.gov/ndic/pubs0/668/marijuan.htm#Top]
[149] Office of National Drug Control Policy, Southwest Border HIDTA Arizona Partnership, "California: Threat Abstract," *Southwest Border: High-Intensity Drug Trafficking Areas*, March 13, 2003.
<http://www.whitehousedrugpolicy.gov/hidta/frames_ca.html>

experienced the greatest number of drug seizures of the three border crossing points in Imperial County. This increase coincides with greater air smuggling activity observed along the Southwest Border.

Authorities seized 226 kilograms of marijuana on all highways in Northern California in 1999. Almost all marijuana seized originated in and was destined for locations in California. Interstate 5, with about 78 percent of the seizures, is the main highway used for transporting marijuana. U.S. Highways 101, 99, and 395 had only a few small seizures each.[150]

The transporters use tractor-trailers and various other vehicles to move the marijuana over Mexico's highways and secondary roads to the Southwest Border.[151] The principal land corridors from Baja California into Southern California continue to be through and between California port of entries. Marijuana is smuggled in commercial and private vehicles and by backpackers. According to the USCS, most marijuana smugglers use the San Ysidro port of entry, followed by Calexico and Otay Mesa. Large shipments have been commingled with legitimate cargo such as wood chips and produce. Multi-hundred-pound shipments of marijuana have been seized from personal vehicles where they were hidden in various compartments and places such as quarter panels and spare tires. Shipments may also be hidden in boxes of clothing.

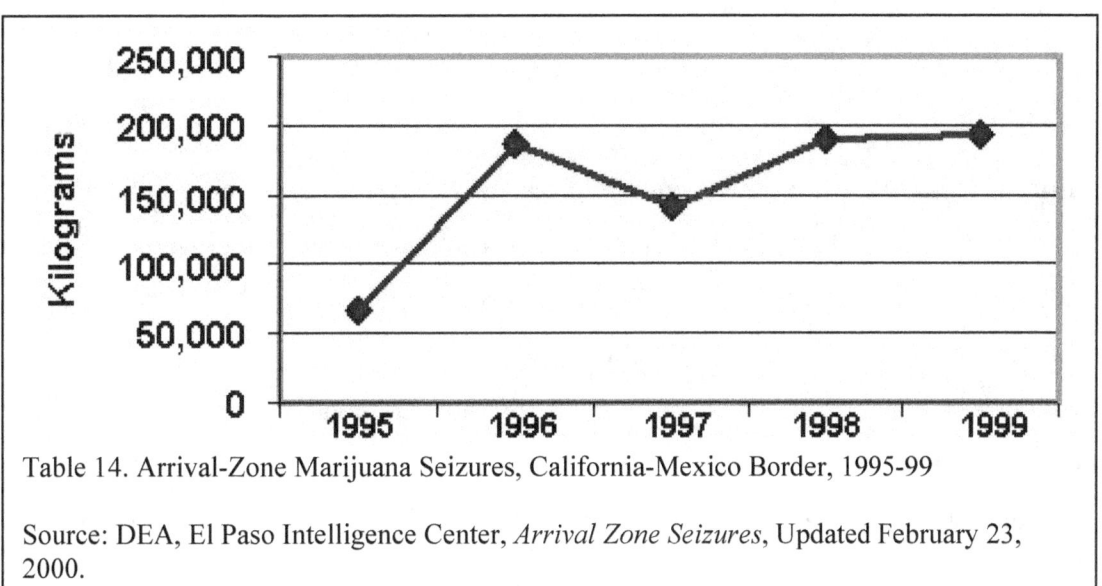

Table 14. Arrival-Zone Marijuana Seizures, California-Mexico Border, 1995-99

Source: DEA, El Paso Intelligence Center, *Arrival Zone Seizures*, Updated February 23, 2000.

---

[150] NDIC, *California Northern and Eastern Districts Drug Threat Assessment*, January 2001.
[151] This paragraph is based on NDIC, *California Southern District Drug Threat Assessment*, Document ID: 2001-S0387SCA-001, May 2002.

The California Border Alliance Group (CBAG) reported in 2002 that marijuana smuggling organizations were moving their operations east of Otay Mountain, and that the majority of seizures were being made west of the Tecate port of entry. The Tierra Del Sol in East San Diego is considered a preferred smuggling area. Backpackers from Mexico can walk across the border, leave the marijuana at a predetermined drop site, and return to Mexico. Pickup vehicles have quick access to Highway 94, which connects to Interstate 8.[152]

The amount of marijuana seized at ports in the Central District increased from FY1998 to FY1999. Port seizures more than doubled from 8,930 pounds to 18,509 pounds over this period. The Port of Los Angeles accounted for the highest volume of marijuana seizures within the Los Angeles area. Activity apparently has shifted to smaller ports within the Los Angeles area. During FY2000, the amount of marijuana seized at the ports of Hueneme and San Luis increased, while that seized at Los Angeles International Airport and the Port of Los Angeles decreased.[153]

Links to Organized Crime: Trafficking organizations operating out of Mexico dominate the market and exploit all means and methods to smuggle Mexican marijuana into Southern California.[154] Mexican cocaine organizations smuggle multi-ton quantities of marijuana into the United States and through the state's Central District.[155]

COLORADO

Marijuana Situation: Marijuana, primarily produced in Mexico, is the most widely available and frequently abused illicit drug in Colorado. It is readily available in multi-pound quantities throughout the state. The highly potent Canadian form of marijuana (BC Bud) is also easily obtainable, although significantly more expensive.

Production: Indoor and outdoor cannabis cultivation is widespread in the state.

Indoor Domestic Grows: Indoor cannabis grows are common, and there have been significant seizures of indoor grows containing 1,000 or more cannabis plants. Indoor operations that utilize

---

[152] This paragraph is based on NDIC, *California Southern District Drug Threat Assessment,* Document ID: 2001-S0387SCA-001, May 2002.
[153] NDIC, *California Central District Drug Threat Assessment*, May 2001.
[154] This paragraph is based on NDIC, *California Southern District Drug Threat* Assessment, Document ID: 2001-S0387SCA-001, May 2002.
[155] NDIC, *California Central District Drug Threat Assessment*, May 2001.

hydroponics to produce high THC sinsemilla are becoming more common. Indoor operations generally are conducted by Caucasian criminal groups and local independent producers.[156]

Outdoor Domestic Grows: Outdoor cannabis cultivation reportedly yields more cannabis than indoor cultivation in Colorado. Mexican criminal groups cultivate large-scale outdoor sites containing thousands of cannabis plants in remote areas of Colorado. Outdoor cannabis operations typically are concealed among legitimate agricultural crops or on remote National Forest Service lands.[157]

Processed and Imported: Most of the marijuana available in the state is imported from Mexico. Marijuana produced in Colorado and other western states, particularly California, by Mexican criminal groups and local independent dealers is available. High-potency marijuana imported from Canada is becoming increasingly available in Colorado's metropolitan areas.[158]

Federal Drug (Marijuana) Seizures, 2002: 43.5 kilograms (DEA). Seizure data reflect the ready availability of marijuana in Colorado. According to FDSS data, federal law enforcement officials in Colorado seized 882.5 kilograms of marijuana in 1998, 901.6 kilograms in 1999, 718.1 kilograms in 2000, and 1,591.5 kilograms in 2001. Law enforcement officials seized 2,348.1 kilograms of marijuana in 1999 and 1,520.9 kilograms in 2000 as part of Operation Pipeline and 175.1 kilograms in 2000 as part of Operation Jetway.[159]

Major Avenues into the State: BC Bud is smuggled into Colorado from British Columbia, Canada, to Washington and Oregon. Bigger loads have been coming in from Mexico. Marijuana typically is transported into the state in commercial trucks, rental and private vehicles, and by package delivery services. Marijuana produced in Mexico or by Mexican criminal groups in Colorado and other western states is distributed primarily by Mexican drug-trafficking organizations and criminal groups at the wholesale level and by Hispanic and African American street gangs at the retail level. Caucasian criminal groups and local independent dealers are the primary distributors of the marijuana and sinsemilla that they produce in Colorado.[160]

Caucasian local independent distributors and a limited number of Mexican criminal groups transport Canada-produced marijuana to Colorado through northwestern states. Marijuana

---

[156] NDIC, Colorado *Drug Threat Assessment Update*, May 2003.
[http://www.usdoj.gov/ndic/pubs4/4300/marijuan.htm#Top]
[157] NDIC, Colorado *Drug Threat Assessment Update*, May 2003.
[158] NDIC, Colorado *Drug Threat Assessment Update*, May 2003.
[159] Most of this paragraph is based on NDIC, Colorado *Drug Threat Assessment Update*, May 2003.
[http://www.usdoj.gov/ndic/pubs4/4300/marijuan.htm#Top]
[160] Most of this paragraph is based on NDIC, Colorado *Drug Threat Assessment Update*, May 2003.

typically is transported into Colorado along the state's interstate highway system. Operation Pipeline data from 2000 indicate that I-25 is the highway most often used to transport marijuana to Colorado, although I-70 also is frequently used. Interstate 76 typically is used to transport marijuana from Colorado to destinations in other states. The Four Corners-Durango area is a major transit area for marijuana being transported from Arizona, California, and New Mexico to cities such as Boston, Chicago, and New York. Commercial, private, and rental vehicles generally are used to transport marijuana into and through the state.[161]

To a much lesser extent, marijuana is also transported by couriers traveling aboard commercial aircraft. BC Bud is transported from British Columbia via Denver International Airport. Couriers on commercial flights also transport marijuana to drug markets in other states via connecting flights through Colorado airports. A small amount of marijuana is transported to Colorado by package delivery services. Marijuana packages typically contain from 5 to 10 pounds of the drug and usually are shipped from Southern California or Texas. The most common cities from which marijuana is transported to Colorado in mail packages are El Paso, Texas; Phoenix, Arizona; and Los Angeles. [162]

Links to Organized Crime: Mexican polydrug-trafficking organizations control the majority of the distribution of marijuana and other drugs in Colorado. African-American and Hispanic street gangs, supplied by Mexican drug-trafficking organizations, also distribute all varieties of marijuana at the retail level. Caucasian local independent dealers distribute locally produced marijuana at the wholesale and retail levels. Caucasian criminal groups in Boulder, Denver, and Jefferson Counties are the primary distributors of BC Bud in Colorado.[163]

CONNECTICUT

Marijuana Situation: Marijuana is the most readily available illicit drug in Connecticut. It can be effortlessly obtained in all areas of the state. It is readily available in the greater New Haven area for individual use and available in multi-ounce/pound quantities for wholesale distribution through Jamaican trafficking groups.

Production:

---

[161] NDIC, Colorado *Drug Threat Assessment Update*, May 2003.
[162] NDIC, Colorado *Drug Threat Assessment Update*, May 2003.
[163] NDIC, Colorado *Drug Threat Assessment Update*, May 2003.

Indoor Domestic Grows: Indoor hydroponic marijuana growth sites are known to be run in suburban areas in New Haven County. These operations are run by a small, tight-knit group that shares technology and growing techniques.

Outdoor Domestic Grows: No information available.

Processed and Imported: Most of the marijuana available in Connecticut is produced in Mexico; however, locally produced marijuana and marijuana imported from Canada also are available.[164]

Federal Drug (Marijuana) Seizures, 2002: 10.1 kilograms.

Major Avenues into the State: Most of the marijuana available in Connecticut is transported from Mexico to southwestern states, then transported to Connecticut primarily via package delivery services.[165] Jamaican traffickers, for example, receive and coordinate the bulk shipment of marijuana packages to the New Haven area from courier services such as the United Parcel Service, Federal Express, and the U.S. Postal Service (Express Mail Delivery).[166] Additional quantities are transported via private and commercial vehicles and couriers aboard commercial aircraft.[167] Caucasian criminal groups smuggle high-quality, Canada-produced marijuana across the U.S.-Canada border primarily via private vehicles and couriers on foot. Couriers on foot typically rendezvous with co-conspirators near the U.S.-Canada border, who then transport the marijuana to Connecticut via private vehicles.

Links to Organized Crime: Mexican criminal groups are the dominant transporters of marijuana into Connecticut; however, Caucasian, Jamaican, and other Hispanic criminal groups as well as crews and local independent dealers of various ethnic backgrounds also transport marijuana into the state.[168] Caucasian, Dominican, Jamaican, Mexican, and other Hispanic criminal groups are the principal wholesale-level distributors of marijuana in Connecticut.

DELAWARE

Marijuana Situation: Marijuana is abundantly available in both wholesale and retail quantities in Delaware. It is the most readily available illicit drug in the state. Higher-quality marijuana is

---

[164] NDIC, *Connecticut Drug Threat Assessment Update*, July 2003.
[http://www.usdoj.gov/ndic/pubs5/5333/marijuan.htm#Top]
[165] NDIC, *Connecticut Drug Threat Assessment Update*, July 2003.
[166] U.S. DEA state data.
[167] The remainder of this paragraph is based on NDIC, *Connecticut Drug Threat Assessment Update*, July 2003.
[168] This paragraph is based on NDIC, *Connecticut Drug Threat Assessment Update*, July 2003.

available, particularly in Newark. Recreational use of marijuana remains popular with high school- and college age-students, but adults remain the predominant users of marijuana, especially in large social gatherings, such as rock concerts. Marijuana is typically smoked in combination with crack cocaine, heroin, and PCP.

Production: Cannabis is cultivated both outdoors and indoors in Delaware. Caucasian local independent dealers and abusers are the primary cannabis cultivators in the state. Cannabis cultivators in Dover and Milford attempt to conceal operations by growing cannabis intermingled with corn plants or indoors in basements or closets.

Indoor Domestic Grows: Common.

Outdoor Domestic Grows: Common.

Processed and Imported: Most of the marijuana available in Delaware is imported from Mexico; however, locally produced marijuana also is available.[169]

Federal Drug (Marijuana) Seizures, 2002: 1.2 kilograms.

Major Avenues into the State: Because of their proximity to major thoroughfares, localities throughout the state remain transshipment points as well as consumer markets. Jamaican criminal groups are the primary transporters of marijuana into the state. African-American and Caucasian local independent dealers and Mexican criminal groups also transport marijuana into the state, although to a lesser extent. Most of the marijuana available in Delaware is transported from Philadelphia and New York City by private vehicles and couriers aboard trains and buses. Some marijuana is transported from Mexico and southwestern states by package delivery services, private vehicles, and commercial trucks.[170]

Links to Organized Crime: At the retail level, Hispanic, African-American, and Caucasian groups, along with some dominant Jamaican organizations, control the marijuana market by distributing bag, ounce, and pound quantities to users across Pennsylvania and Delaware. Jamaican criminal groups are the primary wholesale-level distributors of marijuana in Delaware. These criminal groups often sell multi-pound quantities of marijuana to African-American and Caucasian local independent dealers and local street gangs, who then distribute the drug at the retail level in the state.[171]

---

[169] NDIC, *Delaware Drug Threat Assessment Update*, May 2003.
[http://www.usdoj.gov/ndic/pubs4/4025/marijuan.htm#Top]
[170] NDIC, *Delaware Drug Threat Assessment Update*, May 2003.
[171] Most of this paragraph is based on NDIC, *Delaware Drug Threat Assessment Update*, May 2003.

FLORIDA

Marijuana Situation: Marijuana, both domestically grown and imported, is readily available throughout Florida and is the most widely available and frequently abused illicit drug in the state.

Production: Cannabis plants are cultivated both indoors and outdoors in the state. Although significant quantities of marijuana are produced in Florida, most of the marijuana available in the state is produced in Jamaica or Mexico. Additional quantities of marijuana are produced in other U.S. states—particularly California and southwestern states—as well as in Canada and Colombia. Of all the cannabis plants eradicated in Florida in 2001, 63 percent were cultivated in 12 counties—Alachua, Brevard, Duval, Gadsden, Hillsborough, Holmes, Jackson, Lee, Miami-Dade, Okeechobee, Orange, and Santa Rosa. Both hydroponic marijuana and commercial-grade marijuana are readily available in Florida. Hydroponically produced marijuana is considerably more expensive than commercial-grade marijuana.[172]

Federal, state, and local law enforcement officials indicate that aggressive aerial detection missions and occasional drought conditions have, at least in part, contributed to a shift from large outdoor grows to indoor grows and smaller, more widely dispersed outdoor grows.

Indoor Domestic Grows: Domestic indoor cultivation is a significant industry throughout Florida. Indoor grows in Miami can be found in gated communities and in houses rented specifically for growing.[173] The availability of plant hot houses and large commercial nurseries allow traffickers ready access to the necessary equipment for indoor grow operations, particularly in southwest Florida. The Fort Myers RO reports that growers are aware of federal threshold limits and are growing fewer than 100 plants per grow to reduce the risk of federal penalties. Cuban refugees have become increasingly involved in marijuana grow houses.[174] According to DEA statistics, Florida ranked third after California (113,009 plants) and Washington (25,799 plants) for the number of cannabis plants seized from indoor grows in the United States in 2001.[175]

---

[172] NDIC, *Florida Drug Threat Assessment Update*, Document ID: 2003-S0381FL-001, July 2003. [http://www.usdoj.gov/ndic/pubs5/5169/marijuan.htm#Top]
[173] "Marijuana," *Pulse Check*: Trends in Drug Abuse, Office of National Drug Control Policy, November 2002. [http://www.whitehousedrugpolicy.gov/publications/drugfact/pulsechk/]
[174] "Marijuana," *Pulse Check*: Trends in Drug Abuse, Office of National Drug Control Policy, November 2002. [http://www.whitehousedrugpolicy.gov/publications/drugfact/pulsechk/]
[175] NDIC, *Florida Drug Threat Assessment Update*, July 2003.

Outdoor Domestic Grows: Most of the marijuana available in Florida is produced in Jamaica or Mexico. Significant quantities of marijuana also are produced in Florida and other U.S. states—particularly California and southwestern states—as well as in Canada and Colombia.[176]

Processed and Imported:

Federal Drug (Marijuana) Seizures: 3,145 kilograms in 2002 (DEA). Marijuana was seized more frequently than any other illicit drug in Florida each year from 1997 through 2001. According to FDSS data, the amount of marijuana seized by federal law enforcement officials in Florida fluctuated but decreased overall from 33,439 kilograms in 1997 to 30,184 kilograms in 2001.[177]

Major Avenues into the State: The more than 8,000 miles of Florida coastline and the short distance of 45 miles between The Bahamas and Florida provide unlimited opportunities for drug-trafficking organizations to use maritime conveyances to smuggle drugs. South Florida, specifically Miami-Dade and Broward counties, are still favorite areas of drug traffickers for the smuggling of large quantities of marijuana into the continental United States from South America, Central America, and the Caribbean. Jacksonville and Miami are regional distribution centers for wholesale and retail quantities of marijuana.

Smuggling occurs by various types of maritime conveyances and cargo freighters, as well as by private and commercial aircraft. Miami International Airport (MIA) continues to be the number one airport in the U.S. for international freight and number three in the world for total freight. Additionally, there is a continued shift to ground transportation (e.g., bus, rail, and vehicle) as a means of transporting narcotics throughout the state and to northern destinations. Marijuana is imported into the Jacksonville area from the U.S. Southwest border, Canada, and Jamaica by every available transportation method. The Panhandle region continues to be a transit area for marijuana from Mexico. Seizures continue along Interstate 10 from trucks, rental vehicles, and trailers traveling east into Florida. Mexican commercial grade marijuana continues to be brought into the Orlando area from the southwest border. It is concealed in hidden compartments in passenger cars and large commercial vehicles, in luggage on commercial air flights, or concealed within freight shipments.

---

[176] NDIC, *Florida Drug Threat Assessment Update*, July 2003.
[177] NDIC, *Florida Drug Threat Assessment Update*, July 2003.

Links to Organized Crime: Miami is the primary domestic command and control center for Colombian narcotics traffickers. However, Jamaican and Mexican criminal groups are the most prominent wholesale distributors of marijuana in Florida, with no specific organization or group controlling the majority of wholesale marijuana distribution in the state. The most prominent mid-level and retail distributors of marijuana in the state are Jamaican, Mexican, African-American, Caucasian, Cuban, and other Caribbean criminal groups; local independent African American and Caucasian dealers; and gangs such as Gangster Disciples, Latin Kings, Vice Lords, and Sureños 13.[178]

GEORGIA

Marijuana Situation: Marijuana, the most commonly abused drug in Georgia, is readily available throughout the state.

Production:

Indoor Domestic Grows: Because of DEA's eradication program and the recent drought, some dealers have resorted to indoor cultivation of marijuana.

Outdoor Domestic Grows: Generally, local outdoor cannabis cultivation sites are increasing because of normally ideal growing conditions in the regions.

Processed and Imported: Texas and Arizona are the usual sources of marijuana that is imported from Mexico and ultimately distributed in Georgia. The primary wholesale suppliers of marijuana are Mexican nationals.

Federal Drug (Marijuana) Seizures, 2002: 992 kilograms.

Major Avenues into the State: Because of its location on the I-95 corridor between New York City and Miami, the key wholesale-level drug distribution centers on the East Coast and major drug importation hubs, Georgia is both a final destination point for drug shipments and a smuggling corridor for drugs transported along the East Coast. In addition, Interstate Highways 10 and 20 run directly into Georgia from drug entry points along the Southwest Border and Gulf Coast. With Georgia bordering North Carolina, South Carolina, and Tennessee, Atlanta is the base for several major dealers who maintain trafficking cells in these states. As the largest city in the South and as a hub for all East/West and North/South travel, Atlanta has become an

---

[178] NDIC, *Florida Drug Threat Assessment Update*, July 2003.

important strategic point for drug-trafficking organizations, especially Mexican-based traffickers who hide within legitimate Hispanic enclaves.

Links to Organized Crime:

HAWAII

Marijuana Situation: Marijuana, the second most significant drug threat to the state, is widely available and frequently abused in Hawaii, especially by teenagers. Most marijuana available in Hawaii is produced locally. It is suspected that much of Hawaiian marijuana is exported to the mainland. The availability of marijuana is perceived by the local population as normal. Marijuana is frequently encountered in the public schools among students as young as sixth grade. A recent survey of high school students indicated that 70 percent of the respondents have easy access to marijuana.[179]

Production: The state consistently ranks among the top five in the number of cannabis plants eradicated. On average, from 1995 to 1999 approximately 650,000 plants were eradicated each year in Hawaii. During 2000 law enforcement agencies eradicated fewer than 467,000 plants because Hawaii County did not participate in statewide eradication efforts. Hawaii maintains its status as a "national leader" in the production of high-grade marijuana, such as "Kona Gold." Cannabis grown outdoors in Hawaii contains some of the highest THC levels in the nation because of the optimal growing conditions, nutrient- and mineral-rich volcanic soil, and advances in hybridization techniques. Cannabis cultivators can produce at least two crops per year in Hawaii. Cannabis cultivation and the production of marijuana have become more prevalent in the wake of sugarcane plantation closings that have resulted in a depressed local economy. Local independent growers, primarily Pacific Islanders, cultivate cannabis outdoors year-round. Small, mail-order marijuana operations from the islands to the mainland exist and survive by shipping small quantities through air parcel providers. Marijuana may be shipped to the West Coast in shipping containers marked "household goods," as growers allegedly move to the mainland, although this has not been confirmed.[180]

---

[179] NDIC, *Hawaii Drug Threat Assessment Update*, May 2002.
[http://www.usdoj.gov/ndic/pubs07/998/marijuan.htm#Top]
[180] NDIC, *Hawaii Drug Threat Assessment Update*, May 2002.

Indoor Domestic Grows: Homegrown marijuana, either harvested from sophisticated indoor grows or from outdoor grows, remains a staple for the local demand and for export to the mainland. Medical marijuana certificates are a concern on the islands, where local users are permitted to grow several plants at their residences for personal consumption.

Outdoor Domestic Grows: Cannabis is grown primarily outdoors in Hawaii by Pacific Islander and other local independent cultivators. Although cannabis is cultivated throughout the state, most cannabis cultivation sites are located on the island of Hawaii. More than 80 percent of the plants eradicated in the state in 1999 were on the island of Hawaii. Cannabis also is cultivated on Kauai, Maui, and Molokai. The size of outdoor cannabis plots varies widely, from as few as five plants to as many as several thousand. Growers often use federal and state land for cannabis cultivation to avoid having their personal property seized. The Department of Land and Natural Resources estimates that 70 percent to 80 percent of cannabis cultivation in Hawaii is done on government land, approximately 10 percent on company land previously planted with sugarcane, and the remainder on private land. Growers often cultivate small cannabis plots in remote mountainous areas, making it difficult for law enforcement authorities to locate and eradicate the plants.[181]

Processed and Imported:

Federal Drug (Marijuana) Seizures, 2002: 2.7 kilograms.

Major Avenues into the State: Local independent dealers and, to a lesser extent, Mexican criminal groups transport Hawaii-produced marijuana to the West Coast, primarily California, as well as to Canada and Mexico. Local independent dealers also transport Canada-produced marijuana from the West Coast into Hawaii, and they distribute the drug at the wholesale level. Pacific Islander and other local independent dealers are the primary wholesale and retail distributors of marijuana throughout Hawaii. Occasionally, BC Bud is smuggled to the continental United States from Vancouver and Quebec and transported to Hawaii. Canada-produced marijuana typically is smuggled across the U.S.-Canada border via commercial truck, private vehicle, or courier; however, there have been incidents of BC Bud being smuggled directly from Canada into Hawaii. Marijuana is transported from island to island within the state by courier and package delivery service.[182]

---

[181] NDIC, *Hawaii Drug Threat Assessment Update*, May 2002.
[182] NDIC, *Hawaii Drug Threat Assessment Update*, May 2002.

Links to Organized Crime:

IDAHO

Marijuana Situation: Indoor and outdoor cannabis cultivation is widespread.

Production:

Indoor Domestic Grows: Indoor marijuana cultivation is common.

Outdoor Domestic Grows: Outdoor marijuana cultivation is widespread.

Processed and Imported: Marijuana imported from Mexico is available but not preferred.

Federal Drug (Marijuana) Seizures, 2002: 1.6 kilograms.

Major Avenues into the State: No information available.

Links to Organized Crime: Mexican national polydrug-trafficking organizations control most drug-trafficking organizations in the state.

ILLINOIS

Marijuana Situation: Marijuana is the most widely available and commonly abused illicit drug in Illinois.

Production: Cannabis is cultivated throughout Illinois at indoor and outdoor grow sites.

Indoor Domestic Grows: Indoor grows often are located in residential basements and have intricate lighting systems to stimulate plant growth.

Outdoor Domestic Grows: Outdoor grow sites are located on public or private land and are generally concealed among vegetation or inside fenced yards.

Processed and Imported: Marijuana imported from Mexico is common.

Federal Drug (Marijuana) Seizures, 2002: 1,871.4 kilograms.

Major Avenues into the State: Because of its geographical location and multi-faceted transportation infrastructure, Chicago is the major transportation hub and distribution center for illegal drugs throughout the Midwest. Commercial trucks, passenger vehicles, package delivery services, air packages or couriers, and railways are the most common means traffickers use to transport drugs into Chicago. Mexican drug-trafficking organizations and criminal groups supply most of the marijuana available in Illinois. They transport the marijuana in bulk quantities from

Mexico through southwestern states using commercial vehicles. The marijuana often is intermingled with legitimate cargo such as produce.[183]

Links to Organized Crime: The Illinois Division of the DEA targets Mexico-based polydrug-trafficking organizations for marijuana-trafficking investigations.

INDIANA

Marijuana Situation: Indiana is an active drug transportation and distribution area. Marijuana abuse remains a significant problem within Indiana.

Production: Indoor and outdoor grows are common.

Indoor Domestic Grows: Locally produced marijuana is cultivated throughout Indiana at indoor grow sites. Indoor grows are located in private residences or large barn-type buildings on private land. Indoor grows often are located in residential basements and have intricate lighting systems to stimulate plant growth.

Outdoor Domestic Grows: Locally produced marijuana is cultivated throughout Indiana at outdoor grow sites. These sites are on public or private land, usually in farm fields or near riverbanks, and are generally concealed among vegetation or inside fenced yards.

Processed and Imported: Marijuana produced in Mexico is transported and distributed by Mexican organizations.

Federal Drug (Marijuana) Seizures, 2002: 15.1 kilograms.

Major Avenues into the State: Highway (automobile and trucking) and airline trafficking are the primary means of drug importation, with busing systems as a secondary means. Mexican drug-trafficking organizations transport the marijuana in bulk quantities from Mexico through southwestern states using commercial vehicles. The marijuana often is intermingled with legitimate cargo such as produce. [184]Seven interstate highway systems and 20 U.S. highways provide interstate and intrastate links for drug trafficking, especially with the Southwest Border and California. Transportation is usually by tractor-trailers in multi-hundred pound quantities. The northern part of Indiana lies on Lake Michigan, which is a major waterway within the St. Lawrence Seaway system providing international shipping for all sections of the Midwest.

---

[183] NDIC, *Illinois Drug Threat Assessment Update*, Document ID: 2002-S0382IL-001, May 2002. [http://www.usdoj.gov/ndic/pubs1/1010/marijuan.htm#Top]
[184] NDIC, *Illinois Drug Threat Assessment Update*, May 2002.

Links to Organized Crime: Mexican criminal groups are the primary wholesale distributors of marijuana within Indiana.

IOWA

Marijuana Situation: Both imported and domestic marijuana is readily available in Iowa. "Ditch-weed," which is used as filler for higher-purity imported marijuana, is a continuing problem.[185]

Production:

Indoor Domestic Grows: Small indoor grow operations have been found in eastern and central Iowa.

Outdoor Domestic Grows: Small outdoor grow operations have been found in eastern and central Iowa.

Processed and Imported: The majority of the marijuana is imported from the southwest border with Mexico by motor vehicles, and mail delivery services.

Federal Drug (Marijuana) Seizures, 2002: 5.1 kilograms.

Major Avenues into the State: Iowa serves as a transshipment point for drugs being transported to the eastern United States via Interstate 80. Interstates 29 and 35 also provide a critical north-south transportation avenue for drug traffickers.

Links to Organized Crime:

KANSAS

Marijuana Situation: Marijuana is readily available throughout Kansas. Domestically produced marijuana is available throughout the state, but the imported marijuana from Mexico dominates the market.

Production: Most of the marijuana available in Kansas is produced in Mexico; however, some cannabis also is cultivated throughout the state, primarily by local independent Caucasian growers. Outdoor cannabis cultivation is more common than indoor cultivation. Cannabis is

---

[185] The term "ditch weed" is commonly used to describe wild marijuana.

cultivated both outdoors and indoors in Barton County and in Coffeyville, Garden City, Kansas City, Topeka, and Wichita.[186]

Indoor Domestic Grows: Common.

Outdoor Domestic Grows: In Kansas outdoor cannabis grow sites typically yield more cannabis than indoor sites. Outdoor cannabis growers often conceal cannabis plants to avoid detection by law enforcement authorities. In Lyon County, cultivators place small groups of cannabis plants around utility poles. In Jefferson County camouflage netting is used to conceal cannabis in remote wooded locations.[187]

Processed and Imported: Marijuana, particularly commercial-grade marijuana produced in Mexico, is the most widely available illicit drug in Kansas.[188]

Federal Drug (Marijuana) Seizures: 1,472.1 kilograms in 2002 (DEA). According to FDSS data, federal law enforcement officials in Kansas seized 1,741.3 kilograms in 1998, 3,484.8 kilograms in 1999, 5,827.6 kilograms in 2000, and 2,539.4 kilograms in 2001. Law enforcement authorities that reported to Operation Pipeline seized more than 4,900 kilograms of marijuana in 1999 and over 10,000 kilograms in 2000. Kansas Highway Police seized 7,566 kilograms of marijuana in 2000 and 2,884 kilograms in 2001. In 2001 the Kansas City Police Department seized 488 kilograms of marijuana.[189]

Major Avenues into the State: Marijuana is imported from Mexico through cities on the southwest border and transported in large shipments by the interstate highways through Dallas and Oklahoma City, and on to Kansas City. From Kansas City, the marijuana is further distributed to other cities in Kansas and other states. Kansas is a transshipment point for drugs being transported to the eastern United States via Interstates 35 and 70 from the southwest border and west coast cities. Law enforcement officials in Lawrence, Kansas, just west of Kansas City, are reporting a large influx of high-purity BC Bud marijuana from Canada.

Links to Organized Crime: Mexican criminal groups are the primary transporters of wholesale quantities of Mexico-produced marijuana into Kansas.

---

[186] NDIC, *Kansas Drug Threat Assessment Update*, March 2003.
[187] NDIC, *Kansas Drug Threat Assessment Update*, March 2003.
[188] NDIC, *Kansas Drug Threat Assessment Update*, March 2003.
[189] NDIC, *Kansas Drug Threat Assessment Update*, March 2003.

KENTUCKY

Marijuana Situation: Marijuana is the primary drug threat in the state of Kentucky, which is the site of large-scale marijuana cultivation. Most of the marijuana produced in the state is exported to markets in other states, including Illinois, Ohio, Kentucky, New York, California, Texas, Pennsylvania and Washington D.C. The contrast between marijuana production rates in Kentucky and consumption rates in the state reflects this export trend. Far more marijuana is cultivated in Kentucky than the local market consumes. Additionally, anecdotal information from cities such as Detroit, Philadelphia, Washington D.C., New York City, etc., suggests that Kentucky marijuana is prized in those markets.

Production: Kentucky routinely ranks third or fourth in terms of total marijuana production, after California, Hawaii, and sometimes Tennessee. From 1990 through 2000, the Daniel Boone National Forest, located in eastern Kentucky, has led all national forests for the number of cannabis plants eradicated. In 1999, 38 percent (184,000 plants) of all cannabis eradicated on national forest land was taken from the Daniel Boone National Forest.

Indoor Domestic Grows: Cannabis is more commonly cultivated outdoors in Kentucky, but the number of indoor cannabis grows, including sophisticated hydroponic operations, is increasing throughout Kentucky. According to 1998 DCE/SP statistics, California, Florida, Oregon, Alaska, and Kentucky are the five leading states for indoor cannabis eradication.[190]

Outdoor Domestic Grows: A primary source of marijuana cultivation has been the Eastern Kentucky region in particular, especially the Daniel Boone National Forest, which covers more than 690,000 acres. The forestlands are remote, sparsely populated, very accessible, and fall within what is known as the "marijuana belt," so-named because of ideal soil and climate conditions for cannabis cultivation. Overall, 102,288 marijuana plants were eradicated in the Daniel Boone National Forest in 2002.

The Daniel Boone National Forest is harmed by the collateral effects of marijuana cultivation, which includes property damage to natural resources, archeological sites, and wildlife, including endangered species. Marijuana producers have destroyed numerous trees, plants, and fauna, as well as gates and fences, to clear cultivation sites and drive vehicles to/from the marijuana plots. Additionally, during the cultivation of marijuana, growers frequently use a

---

[190] NDIC, *Kentucky Drug Threat Assessment Update*, July 2002.
[http://www.usdoj.gov/ndic/pubs1/1540/marijuan.htm#Top]

variety of poisonous chemical fertilizers upon forestlands. In 2002, 136 acres of the Daniel Boone National Forest were classified by the U.S. Forest Service as "impacted environmentally because of drug activity."

Processed and Imported: Marijuana imported from Mexico is common.

Federal Drug (Marijuana) Seizures, 2002: 6.3 kilograms.

Major Avenues into the State: Mexican criminal groups are the primary transporters of Mexico-produced marijuana into Kentucky, which they usually transport through California and southwestern states. Mexico-produced marijuana is transported across the U.S.-Mexico border, then north to I-40 and I-70. Marijuana also is transported through Kentucky in airline cargo.[191]

Links to Organized Crime: The same Mexican criminal groups that transport Mexico-produced marijuana into Kentucky distribute it at the wholesale level. These groups usually sell the marijuana to local Caucasian independent dealers, who are the dominant retail distributors of Mexico-produced marijuana.[192]

LOUSIANA

Marijuana Situation: Marijuana is the most widely available illicit drug in Louisiana, and homegrown marijuana is an important element of the illegal drug threat in the state.

Production: Marijuana produced locally and in neighboring states is readily available. Louisiana provides an adequate environment for cannabis cultivation. The growing season extends for most of the year because of the state's generally temperate climate. Cannabis is sometimes intermixed with other crops, making it visible only from the air.

Indoor Domestic Grows: The availability of high-grade domestically produced marijuana has increased as a result of modern techniques of indoor cultivation (i.e., the use of cloning and hydroponics to increase the potency).

Outdoor Domestic Grows: Outdoor cannabis cultivation appears to be decreasing in Louisiana because of the widespread availability of inexpensive Mexico-produced marijuana, increased eradication efforts, and recent droughts.[193]

---

[191] NDIC, *Kentucky Drug Threat Assessment Update*, July 2002.
[192] NDIC, *Kentucky Drug Threat Assessment Update*, July 2002.
[193] NDIC, *Lousiana Drug Threat Assessment Update*, May 2001.
[http://www.usdoj.gov/ndic/pubs0/666/marijuan.htm#Top]

Processed and Imported: Most marijuana available in Louisiana is produced in Mexico. Louisiana's proximity to Texas and the Southwest Border ensures a steady supply of Mexico-produced marijuana, which is inexpensive in large part because of its low THC content (average 3.3 percent).[194]

Federal Drug (Marijuana) Seizures, 2002: 46.7 kilograms.

Major Avenues into the State: Conventional drugs such as marijuana comprise the bulk of drugs shipped through and arriving in Louisiana. Overland transportation utilizing private and commercial vehicles is the most commonly encountered smuggling method in Louisiana. Colombian, Mexican, and Caribbean traffickers traveling to and from Miami, Houston, or the Southwest Border via I-10, I-12, I-20 (East / West routes) and Interstate 55 (North / South route) are largely responsible for the transportation and distribution of marijuana into Louisiana. Additionally, regional and local drug-trafficking organizations ensure widespread availability throughout the state. In many regions of Louisiana, the price of marijuana has been decreasing because of the availability of Mexico-produced marijuana transported from hub cities in Texas (Houston, Dallas, San Antonio, Brownsville, and El Paso). A common practice among distributors is to "bulk up" domestic marijuana with less expensive, lower-quality, Mexico-produced marijuana to increase profits

Links to Organized Crime: Mexican drug-trafficking organizations clearly dominate the greatest portion of wholesale distribution through Texas into Louisiana, but Colombian and Caribbean traffickers are also actively involved. Local independent dealers, street gangs, and some small ethnic drug-trafficking groups dominate domestic marijuana retail distribution.

MAINE

Marijuana Situation: Marijuana, locally grown and imported from Canada, Massachusetts, and New York, is the primary drug of abuse in Maine. Marijuana is plentiful and readily available. Hashish is available sporadically in small quantities, but the increasing popularity of hashish in Canada may change the hashish situation in Maine. Traffickers have moved hashish and hash oil through Maine and into Canada.

---

[194] NDIC, *Lousiana Drug Threat Assessment Update*, May 2001.

Production: Marijuana growing in the Portland area continues to become more sophisticated, with new seedlings moved indoors for the winter and then moved outdoors again in the spring.[195]

Indoor Domestic Grows: Year-round indoor grows are common.

Outdoor Domestic Grows: No information available.

Processed and Imported: Most of the marijuana available in Maine is produced in Mexico; however, locally produced marijuana and high-grade marijuana produced in Canada also are available. Commercial-grade marijuana is often obtained from middlemen in the southern New England states and New York. Caucasian traffickers typically supply locally grown marijuana as well as marijuana shipped from the southwest border and Canada. Shipments ranging from 15 to 500 pounds typically enter the state via Interstate 95 in automobiles, campers, rental trucks, and tractor-trailers.

Federal Drug (Marijuana) Seizures, 2002: 5.8 kilograms.

Major Avenues into the State: Caucasian criminal groups, local independent dealers, and organized motorcycle gangs are the primary transporters of marijuana into Maine. They transport the drug from southwestern states, Massachusetts, and Canada primarily via private and commercial vehicles and package delivery services. Canada-produced marijuana also is smuggled across the U.S.-Canada border into Maine by couriers on foot, snowmobiles, or all-terrain vehicles. Upon entering the United States, the couriers usually rendezvous with co-conspirators who transport the drug to its final destination via private vehicles.[196] Interstate 95 provides an important north-south transportation route for traffickers traveling most frequently to sources of drug supply in several northeastern Massachusetts cities. Additionally, Maine's 228 miles of coastline and 3,478 miles of shoreline offer ample opportunities for smugglers.

Links to Organized Crime: Motorcycle groups control much of the marijuana distribution in Maine, using associates to distribute approximately 300 to 500 pounds monthly.

MARYLAND

Marijuana Situation: The most widely abused drug in Maryland, marijuana remains easily available in every part of the state. Low levels of marijuana cultivation occur in the state,

---

[195] "Marijuana," *Pulse Check*: Trends in Drug Abuse, Office of National Drug Control Policy, November 2002. [http://www.whitehousedrugpolicy.gov/publications/drugfact/pulsechk/]
[196] NDIC, *Maine Drug Threat Assessment Update*, August 2003. [http://www.usdoj.gov/ndic/pubs5/5764/marijuan.htm#Top]

primarily in western Maryland and along the Eastern Shore, where private farmland and public parkland are conducive to growers' concerns for anonymity.

Production: Marijuana produced in Maryland is available to a lesser extent than Mexican-produced marijuana. Cannabis is cultivated both indoors and outdoors within the state. Local independent dealers, primarily Caucasians, cultivate cannabis and dominate retail distribution of all types of marijuana in Maryland.[197]

Indoor Domestic Grows: Indoor cultivation is increasing because the quality of the marijuana obtained from indoor grows tends to be higher and the drug commands a higher price.

Outdoor Domestic Grows: Outdoor cultivation is common during the summer months, especially on the Eastern Shore. In Caroline County on the Eastern Shore, the Sheriff's Office reported in 2000 that most of the marijuana sold in its jurisdiction was locally grown, primarily outdoors.

Processed and Imported: Most of the marijuana available in Maryland is produced in Mexico.

Federal Drug (Marijuana) Seizures: 13.9 kilograms, 2002 (DEA). According to FDSS data, federal law enforcement agencies in Maryland seized 224.5 kilograms of marijuana in 1998, 323.3 kilograms in 1999, and 394.4 kilograms in 2000.[198]

Major Avenues into the State: Some of the marijuana consumed in Maryland is produced within the state, but most is produced in Mexico and transshipped through California and southwestern states. Jamaican criminal groups are the dominant transporters of marijuana into Maryland; Mexican criminal groups transport lesser amounts into the state. Jamaican criminal groups usually purchase marijuana from Mexican criminal groups in the southwestern United States and transport it primarily via package delivery services into Maryland, although transportation by automobile, bus, and airline does occur.[199]

Maryland is situated on the north end of the mid-Atlantic region and bisected by Interstate-95. Drugs, weapons, and illicit proceeds destined for points south of New York City routinely transit the state through Baltimore. Maryland's drug situation is complicated by the presence of two major metropolitan areas in the state: Baltimore and its surrounding counties in the northern part of the state, and the suburban counties of Washington, DC in southern

---

[197] NDIC, *Maryland Drug Threat Assessment Update*, August 2002.
[198] NDIC, *Maryland Drug Threat Assessment Update*, August 2002.
[http://www.usdoj.gov/ndic/pubs1/1827/index.htm]
[199] NDIC, *Maryland Drug Threat Assessment Update*, August 2002.

Maryland. In addition, Maryland's major seaport in Baltimore contributes to a substantial amount of international drug traffic coming into the state.

Links to Organized Crime: Jamaican and Mexican organized crime groups are involved.

MASSACHUSETTS

Marijuana Situation: Marijuana is the most readily available illicit drug in Massachusetts.

Production: Domestically grown marijuana is found in all areas of Massachusetts, from the extreme western part of the state all the way out to Nantucket Island.

Indoor Domestic Grows: In the past few years, the state has seen an increase in the marijuana cultivated indoors hydroponically as well as an increase in the size of the plants and their THC levels.

Outdoor Domestic Grows: No information available.

Processed and Imported: Most of the marijuana available in Massachusetts is produced in Mexico.

Federal Drug (Marijuana) Seizures: 13.9 kilograms, 2002 (DEA). FDSS data indicate that federal law enforcement officials in Massachusetts seized 78.5 kilograms of marijuana in 2002.[200]

Major Avenues into the State: Most marijuana in the state originates in Mexico or the Southwestern United States. However, marijuana of both Colombian and Jamaican origin has been encountered, and most of the Boston area's marijuana comes from Canada.[201] The majority of the marijuana in Massachusetts is imported from the southwest border with Mexico by aircraft, land vehicles, and delivery services. Personal-use quantities of hashish continue to arrive in Boston on flights from the Netherlands and other source countries.

Links to Organized Crime: Mexican criminal groups are the dominant transporters of marijuana into Massachusetts. Caucasian, Dominican, Jamaican, and Hispanic criminal groups

---

[200] NDIC, *Massachusetts Drug Threat Assessment Update, 2003 Update*, May 2003.
[http://www.usdoj.gov/ndic/pubs3/3980/index.htm]
[201] "Marijuana," *Pulse Check*: Trends in Drug Abuse, Office of National Drug Control Policy, November 2002.
[http://www.whitehousedrugpolicy.gov/publications/drugfact/pulsechk/]

are the principal wholesale-level distributors of marijuana in the state.[202] The Hell's Angels group controls the importation of the Boston area's marijuana from Canada.[203]

MICHIGAN

Marijuana Situation: Marijuana is the most commonly used and readily available illicit drug throughout the state of Michigan. It is popular among every racial and ethnic group in the region and is particularly popular among high school students.

Production: Domestically grown marijuana is available and may even be grown for export to other near-by states and Canada.

Indoor Domestic Grows: No information available.

Outdoor Domestic Grows: No information available.

Processed and Imported: The vast majority of marijuana sold in Michigan originates in Mexico, but high-grade marijuana comes from Canada.

Federal Drug (Marijuana) Seizures, 2002: 529 kilograms.

Major Avenues into the State: No information available.

Links to Organized Crime: Mexican organized crime groups are involved in supplying the state's Mexican marijuana.

On September 19, 2003, authorities seized this 2000 GMC cargo van, which had been converted into a homemade armored vehicle by marijuana traffickers in Detroit.

Source: DEA

Individuals of Vietnamese decent are growing high-grade marijuana in rental houses in Ontario, Canada, and using trucks hauling trash from Ontario into Michigan to smuggle marijuana into the United States and cash back into Canada.

---

[202] NDIC, *Massachusetts Drug Threat Assessment Update, 2003 Update*, May 2003.
[203] "Marijuana," *Pulse Check*: Trends in Drug Abuse, Office of National Drug Control Policy, November 2002. [http://www.whitehousedrugpolicy.gov/publications/drugfact/pulsechk/]

MINNESOTA

Marijuana Situation: Marijuana is the most commonly used and readily available drug in Minnesota.

Production: Marijuana is readily available from local cultivators.

Indoor Domestic Grows: Common.

Outdoor Domestic Grows: Common.

Processed and Imported: Marijuana imported from Mexico is common.

Federal Drug (Marijuana) Seizures, 2002: 9.5 kilograms.

Major Avenues into the State: Mexican drug-trafficking organizations and criminal groups are the primary transporters of marijuana into the state. According to the Minneapolis Police Department, bulk marijuana shipments are smuggled across the U.S.-Mexico Border to southwestern states such as Arizona and Texas and then divided into smaller loads of up to 500 pounds. The smaller loads are then transported to Minnesota by private vehicle. Marijuana is also transported into the state via package delivery services, as evidenced by recent seizures. Marijuana also is transported into the state from Canada, although there have been no major recent seizures.[204]

Links to Organized Crime: In Minnesota, Mexican drug-trafficking organizations control the transportation, distribution, and bulk sales of marijuana. Numerous Mexican groups and street gangs such as the Latin Kings are operating in the state. As a general rule, the upper echelon Mexican distributors in Minnesota transport the majority of their proceeds back to family members residing in Mexico. At the retail level, independent African-American traffickers, African-American street gangs, Native-American gangs, and independent white groups purchase marijuana from Mexican traffickers.

MISSISSIPPI

Marijuana Situation: The drug of choice and most widely abused drug among consumers in Mississippi is marijuana. Marijuana is trafficked and used by all ethnic and socioeconomic groups in Mississippi.

Production:

---

[204] NDIC, *Minnesota Drug Threat Assessment Update,* June 2002.
[http://www.usdoj.gov/ndic/pubs1/1158/marijuan.htm#Top]

Indoor Domestic Grows: No information available.

Outdoor Domestic Grows: Domestically cultivated marijuana is available throughout Northern Mississippi in patches of four to five plants in and around dense vegetation on United States forestry land and around area lakes.

Processed and Imported:

Federal Drug (Marijuana) Seizures, 2002: 294.4 kilograms.

Major Avenues into the State: The movement of illegal drugs into and through Mississippi has been a significant problem for law enforcement for a number of years. Mississippi is ideally suited with its interstate system, deepwater and river ports, and air and rail systems as the "Crossroads of the South" to facilitate drug movement from the South Texas/Mexico area and Gulf ports to the entire mid west and eastern seaboard of the United States. Drug-trafficking patterns indicate the interstate highway system to be the preferred method of transporting illegal drugs into and through Mississippi. Large quantities of Mexican marijuana are transported from Texas through Mississippi on interstates 10, 12, and 55 destined for larger cities in the Northeastern and Southeastern United States. Couriers in pick-up trucks, vans, tractor-trailers and buses transport the marijuana in 50, 100 and 200 pound quantities in concealed compartments. Proceeds from the drug sales are returned in the same manner.

Links to Organized Crime:

MISSOURI

Marijuana Situation: Marijuana is readily available throughout the state, with Mexican marijuana being imported from the Southwest Border.

Production:

Indoor Domestic Grows: Indoor marijuana growing continues to increase.

Outdoor Domestic Grows: No information available.

Processed and Imported: Marijuana imported from Mexico is common.

Federal Drug (Marijuana) Seizures, 2002: 28.8 kilograms.

Major Avenues into the State:

Links to Organized Crime: Mexican polydrug-trafficking organizations control a large majority of the distribution of marijuana in Missouri.

MONTANA

Marijuana Situation: Marijuana is readily available throughout Montana, and is the most commonly abused illegal drug in the state. A recent survey conducted by the Montana State Addictive and Mental Disorders Division indicated that 47 percent of all high school students had used marijuana in their lifetime. The survey also found that 27 percent described themselves as regular users.

Production:

Indoor Domestic Grows: Locally produced marijuana is primarily grown indoors, with grows generally consisting of fewer than 100 plants.

Outdoor Domestic Grows: No information available.

Processed and Imported: Marijuana imported from Mexico is common.

Federal Drug (Marijuana) Seizures, 2002: 7.7 kilograms.

Major Avenues into the State: The majority of the marijuana consumed in Montana originates in Mexico. Mexican polydrug-trafficking organizations transport marijuana in vehicles from the southwest border states to Montana. Trafficking groups normally acquire supplies of marijuana from the Southwest Border area and smuggle hundred-pound loads into Montana on a monthly or bi-monthly basis. Potent B.C. Bud or Kind Bud from the Pacific Northwest and Western Canada is increasing in popularity and availability. B.C. Bud is often smuggled directly into Montana across the Canadian border. This marijuana would then be transshipped to other areas of the United States.

Links to Organized Crime: Mexican polydrug-trafficking organizations.

NEBRASKA[205]

Marijuana Situation: Marijuana is the most prevalent and frequently abused illicit drug in Nebraska. Most of the marijuana available in the state is produced in Mexico, although some cannabis is cultivated locally.

Production: A large percentage of locally cultivated cannabis is grown outdoors; however, cannabis growers increasingly are using sophisticated indoor cultivation operations. Domestic production of both outdoor and hydroponic indoor grows have been steady, with many seizures

---

[205] This section is based largely on NDIC, *Nebraska Drug Threat Assessment*, Document ID: 2003-S0389NE-001, July 2003. <http://www.usdoj.gov/ndic/pubs4/4934/index.htm>

netting upwards of 500 plants. Caucasian local independent dealers are the primary cannabis cultivators in the state. Cannabis is cultivated both indoors and outdoors in Lincoln, Norfolk, and Omaha.

Indoor Domestic Grows: Plants are increasingly cultivated indoors because they generally yield high potency marijuana, which sells for a higher price.

Outdoor Domestic Grows: In Nebraska, outdoor cannabis cultivation sites typically have more than twice as many cannabis plants per site as indoor operations. Cultivators in western Nebraska occasionally intermingle cannabis plants with corn crops, in an effort to avoid detection by law enforcement authorities. Some growers use the land of unsuspecting farmers and plant cannabis throughout the field to minimize the risk of detection. Cannabis growers often cultivate a hybrid plant that does not grow as tall as corn plants and, therefore, remains well hidden from landowners and authorities.

Processed and Imported:

Seizure Data: Seizure data reflect the ready availability of marijuana in Nebraska. According to FDSS data, federal law enforcement officials in Nebraska seized 339 kilograms in 1998, 2,120 kilograms in 1999, 1,335 kilograms in 2000, and 438 kilograms in 2001. Law enforcement authorities that reported to Operation Pipeline seized more than 2,501 kilograms in 1999 and more than 1,009 kilograms in 2000. The Omaha Police Department seized almost 497 kilograms of marijuana in 2001.

Federal Drug (Marijuana) Seizures, 2002: 0.1 kilograms.

Major Avenues into the State: Mexican criminal groups are the primary transporters of wholesale quantities of Mexico-produced marijuana into Nebraska from Mexico, California, and southwestern states in private and commercial vehicles. Mexican criminal groups also recruit individuals to transport marijuana to Nebraska from these locations. A common route used to transport marijuana is I-15, which traverses Southern California, Nevada, and the northwestern corner of Arizona, then connects with I-80 in northern Utah. Interstate 80 provides easy west-to-east access across the state. Transporters usually use I-80 to haul marijuana destined for other states through Nebraska. They frequently travel from California and southwestern states through Nebraska along I-80 en route to destinations in Michigan, Minnesota, and Ohio. Marijuana typically is transported to Nebraska in hidden compartments within private and commercial vehicles, as well as being concealed in boxes, metal containers, duffel bags, and suitcases.

Links to Organized Crime: Marijuana produced outside of Nebraska and transported into the state is controlled by Mexican drug-trafficking organizations at the wholesale level. Mexican criminal groups and, to a lesser extent, local independent dealers are the primary wholesale and retail marijuana distributors in the state.

NEVADA

Marijuana Situation: Domestically cultivated and Mexican-grown marijuana remains readily available in Nevada

Production:

Indoor Domestic Grows: There was an increased prevalence of indoor marijuana cultivation in the Las Vegas area during 2002. Growers are using elaborate hydroponic equipment to cultivate high-grade marijuana.

Outdoor Domestic Grows: No information available.

Processed and Imported: Marijuana imported from Mexico is common.

Federal Drug (Marijuana) Seizures, 2002: 0.9 kilograms.

Major Avenues into the State: Because of its close proximity to California and its porous border, Nevada often serves as a transshipment point for various drugs to the central and eastern sections of the United States. Mexican marijuana arrives in Nevada primarily from California by ground transport.

Links to Organized Crime: Mexican polydrug-trafficking organizations are still the primary source of marijuana smuggled into the area.

NEW HAMPSHIRE

Marijuana Situation: Marijuana is the most widely abused and readily available illicit drug in New Hampshire. The percentage of New Hampshire residents aged 12 or older who reported having abused marijuana in the past month (6.0 percent) was higher than the percentage nationwide (4.8 percent), according to the 1999 and 2000 National Household Survey on Drug Abuse.[206]

---

[206] NDIC, *New Hampshire Drug Threat Assessment Update*, May 2003.
[http://www.usdoj.gov/ndic/pubs4/4123/marijuan.htm]

Production: Domestically produced marijuana is available in New Hampshire, though not as readily in recent years. Cannabis is cultivated both outdoors and indoors in New Hampshire. Caucasian local independent dealers and abusers are the primary cannabis cultivators in the state.

Indoor Domestic Grows: Common.

Outdoor Domestic Grows: Because of the rural nature of the state, particularly the northern two thirds, the potential growing areas are limitless, and most of the outdoor growers have reduced the size of their plots and increased the variety and scope of their concealment efforts.

Processed and Imported: High-potency, Canadian-grown marijuana is readily available in New Hampshire. This high-potency, Canadian-grown marijuana's THC content can range from 15 percent to as much as 25 percent. THC content in excess of 22 percent has been seen in the state. Most of the marijuana available in New Hampshire, however, is produced in Mexico.[207]

Federal Drug (Marijuana) Seizures, 2002: 0 kilograms.

Major Avenues into the State: For the past several years, almost all foreign-origin marijuana encountered in New Hampshire originated in Mexico. Local Caucasian independent dealers travel weekly or bi-monthly to Arizona and Southern California to obtain 200- to 300-pound quantities of the drug. The marijuana is usually transported into the state by land vehicle. Marijuana is also being shipped in relatively small quantities (20 to 50-pound packages) into the state, often directly from southwestern states, utilizing U. S. and other mail services. The dealers and criminal groups typically travel to Lowell and Lawrence, Massachusetts, in private vehicles to purchase marijuana from individuals and criminal groups of various ethnic backgrounds for retail-level distribution in New Hampshire.[208] High-quality, Canada-produced marijuana is smuggled across the U.S.-Canada border via private vehicles, snowmobiles, all-terrain vehicles, and by couriers on foot. These smugglers typically rendezvous in New Hampshire with members of their criminal group, who transport the drug to its final destination via private vehicle.

Links to Organized Crime: Mexican organized crime groups are involved.

NEW JERSEY

Marijuana Situation: Marijuana is the most widely available and frequently abused illicit drug in the state.

---

[207] NDIC, *New Hampshire Drug Threat Assessment Update*, May 2003.
[208] The remainder of this paragraph is based on NDIC, *New Hampshire Drug Threat Assessment Update*, May 2003.

Production: Cannabis is cultivated both indoors and outdoors throughout rural New Jersey, particularly in Atlantic, Cumberland, Gloucester, and Warren counties.

Indoor Domestic Grows: Indoor grows often are located in private residences. Indoor marijuana grows are usually encountered in the southern rural areas of the state, where detection is more difficult. It also is cultivated indoors in metropolitan areas of the state.

Outdoor Domestic Grows: Rural areas of the state provide the opportunity for outdoor grows. Cannabis plants often are hidden in farmers' fields by replacing corn plants with cannabis plants or by planting the cannabis between the rows of corn.

Processed and Imported: The majority of the marijuana encountered in the state is of Mexican origin, although Jamaican and Canadian marijuana has also been seen, but on a much lesser scale.

Federal Drug (Marijuana) Seizures: 1.1 kilograms, 2002 (DEA). Marijuana is the most frequently seized illicit drug in New Jersey, constituting almost 60 percent of the total illicit drugs seized by federal law enforcement officials in the state from 1999 through 2001.[209]

Major Avenues into the State: The so-called "crossroads of the east" and gateway state, New Jersey is an ideal strategic corridor as well as a vulnerable corridor for transportation of drug contraband and illicit currency between the major industrial markets of New York and Philadelphia, with major interstate highways, roadways, international airports/seaports, and other arteries capable of accommodating voluminous amounts of passenger and cargo traffic. Criminal groups and local independent dealers in at least two states, New York and Pennsylvania, transport marijuana into New Jersey. Typically, marijuana is transported to the New Jersey area by automobiles, tractor-trailers, vessels, U.S. Postal Service, overnight services, parcel post, and commercial air from Southwest Border States. Most of the marijuana seizures in the state have occurred at Newark Liberty International Airport, where passengers from Southwest Border states attempt to smuggle marijuana, which is usually wrapped in cellophane and placed within luggage. Additionally, bulk packages, normally weighing between 10 to 50 pounds each, arrive daily at parcel/cargo services. Although hashish is rarely encountered in the state, more than 565 kilograms being shipped from India to Detroit were seized in October 2002.

---

[209] NDIC, *New Jersey Drug Threat Assessment Update*, August 2002.
[http://www.usdoj.gov/ndic/pubs1/1703/marijuan.htm#Top]

Most marijuana available in New Jersey, particularly in Newark, originates in Mexico and Jamaica. Marijuana produced in Mexico frequently is smuggled in multi-ton shipments inside tractor-trailers from California and southwestern states into New Jersey. Marijuana produced in Jamaica usually is smuggled into New Jersey in commercial maritime vessels and aircraft and through express mail services. Some marijuana produced in Jamaica is smuggled in maritime vessels to other U.S. states and then transported in private and commercial vehicles into New Jersey.[210]

Links to Organized Crime: Although Jamaica- and Mexico-based criminal groups are dominant marijuana transporters and distributors, no particular criminal group or independent dealer controls the transportation of marijuana into New Jersey or its distribution within the state.[211]

NEW MEXICO

Marijuana Situation: Marijuana is the most readily available and most commonly abused drug in New Mexico. Marijuana smuggled from Mexico is available from a multitude of sources in both New Mexico and West Texas and is the most prevalent drug in New Mexico. Domestic cannabis eradication programs have led to an increase of over 200 percent in marijuana seizures over the past three years (see Table 15).

Production: Cannabis is cultivated in the state by local independent growers.

Indoor Domestic Grows: Although indoor cannabis cultivation is practiced in New Mexico, hydroponic systems are uncommon. Cannabis cultivated indoors in New Mexico typically is intended for personal consumption.

Outdoor Domestic Grows: Outdoor cannabis cultivation is more common than indoor cultivation. The climate and vast, sparsely populated rural areas of New Mexico create a suitable environment for outdoor cannabis cultivation. Outdoor growers often cultivate cannabis among natural vegetation in an effort to conceal the crop.[212]

---

[210] NDIC, *New Jersey Drug Threat Assessment Update*, August 2002.
[211] NDIC, *New Jersey Drug Threat Assessment Update*, August 2002.
[212] NDIC, *New Mexico Drug Threat Assessment Update*, April 2002.
<http://www.usdoj.gov/ndic/pubs07/803/marijuan.htm#Top>

Processed and Imported: Most of the marijuana available in the state is produced in Mexico; however, some locally produced marijuana also is available. Marijuana loads seized from private vehicles and semi-tractor-trailers range from 500 to 8,000 pounds.

Federal Drug (Marijuana) Seizures, 2002: 10,912.4 kilograms.

Major Avenues into the State: Mexico-produced marijuana typically is transported to New Mexico from Ciudad Juarez and Palomas, Mexico; El Paso, Texas; Phoenix, Arizona; and Los Angeles, California. The principal marijuana smuggling routes include I-10, I-25, I-40, US 54, US 84, and SR-9.[213]

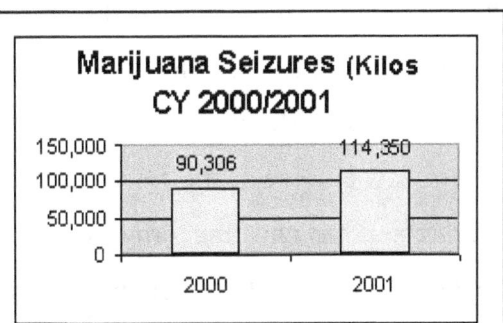

Table 15. New Mexico Marijuana Seizures, 2000-01

Source: Office of National Drug Control Policy

Links to Organized Crime: Mexican drug-trafficking organizations and Mexican criminal groups dominate the transportation and wholesale distribution of Mexico-produced marijuana throughout the state. Local independent dealers control the wholesale distribution of locally produced marijuana. Mexican criminal groups, street gangs, and local independent dealers are the primary retail distributors of Mexico- and locally produced marijuana throughout New Mexico.[214] The largest drug threat in New Mexico is the transshipment of drugs and drug proceeds by Mexican drug-trafficking organizations, which have also established local polydrug distribution organizations that are capable of distributing multiple kilogram quantities locally and regionally.

NEW YORK

Marijuana Situation: Marijuana is the most widely available and frequently abused illicit drug in New York.

Production: A limited amount of cannabis is cultivated locally, especially in Upstate New York. Cannabis plants are cultivated both indoors and outdoors in the state. However, the trend has

---

[213] NDIC, *New Mexico Drug Threat Assessment Update*, April 2002.
[214] NDIC, *New Jersey Drug Threat Assessment Update*, April 2002.
[http://www.usdoj.gov/ndic/pubs07/803/marijuan.htm#Top]

shifted from large outdoor grows to indoor grows and smaller, more widely dispersed outdoor grows.[215]

Indoor Domestic Grows: Common.

Outdoor Domestic Grows: Common.

Processed and Imported: Most of the marijuana available in the state is produced in other U.S. states or in Mexico, Jamaica, or Canada.

Federal Drug (Marijuana) Seizures: 382.8 kilograms, 2002 (DEA). According to FDSS data, federal law enforcement officials in New York seized more marijuana (approximately 16,677 kilograms) than any other drug except cocaine from 1998 through 2001. The annual amount seized fluctuated but was relatively stable from 1998 (2,852 kilograms) through 2001 (2,713 kilograms). According to EPIC Arrival Zone Seizure Statistics, law enforcement officials in New York seized approximately 10,089 kilograms of marijuana transported on commercial aircraft from 1997 through 2001.[216]

Major Avenues into the State: Most of the marijuana entering the New York City area, and some upstate regions, appears to be arriving by air freight or auto/truck transport from Florida or the southwestern United States. Significant amounts also arrive by commercial overnight package services. Upstate regions receive marijuana from the Southwestern United States, and there are continuous reports of local indoor grow operations. Canada is also a source for a significant quantity of marijuana entering New York State.

Links to Organized Crime: Jamaican criminal groups are the most prominent wholesale distributors of marijuana in New York. They are also the primary mid-level and retail marijuana distributors in New York. However, no specific organization or group controls the distribution of marijuana. Mexican criminal groups, members of traditional organized crime, and members of outlaw motorcycle gangs such as Hells Angels also distribute wholesale quantities of marijuana in New York. Traditional organized crime members distribute significant wholesale and midlevel quantities of marijuana in the New York City area.[217]

---

[215] NDIC, *New York Drug Threat Assessment*, November 2002.
[216] NDIC, *New York Drug Threat Assessment*, November 2002.
[http://www.usdoj.gov/ndic/pubs2/2580/marijuan.htm#Top]
[217] NDIC, *New York Drug Threat Assessment*, November 2002.

NORTH CAROLINA

Marijuana Situation: Marijuana is one of the most prevalent drugs in North Carolina and its availability is increasing in part because of smuggling operations by Mexican trafficking organizations into the state directly from Mexico and in part because of ever-larger amounts being smuggled into the state by campers, pickup trucks, and larger vehicles. Marijuana is one of the illicit drugs most commonly transported and distributed by traffickers from Mexico, who hide within ethnic Mexican communities.

Production: Cannabis cultivation is widespread in North Carolina. Outdoor cannabis cultivation is more common than indoor cultivation because of the state's long growing season, temperate climate, and rural areas that allow growers to conceal cultivation sites. During the 2000-2002 period, DCE/SP (Domestic Cannabis Eradication Suppression Program) authorities seized domestically grown marijuana in increasing quantities.[218]

Indoor Domestic Grows: Growers also cultivate high-potency cannabis in indoor hydroponic operations. Indoor grows vary in size and number from dozens to several hundred cannabis plants. Indoor cultivation requires the grower to regulate light, heat, humidity, and fertilizer. Using hydroponic techniques, Caucasian and African-American independent producers are the primary cultivators of cannabis.[219]

Outdoor Domestic Grows: Cannabis growers frequently use federal forestland, particularly in western North Carolina, to minimize the risk of personal property seizures if the plots are seized by law enforcement. Mexican and Caucasian criminal groups are the primary cultivators of outdoor cannabis. Reporting from law enforcement officials indicates that cannabis cultivation is widespread in areas, including the Pisgah and Nantahala national forests in the western part of the state. Outdoor cultivation sites in North Carolina are larger than before, according to law enforcement authorities.[220]

Processed and Imported: Marijuana imported from Mexico is common.

Federal Drug (Marijuana) Seizures: 0.5 kilograms, 2002 (DEA). The amount of marijuana seized in the state increased dramatically from 1998 through 2001. Federal law enforcement

---

[218] NDIC, *North Carolina Drug Threat Assessment*, April 2003.
[http://www.usdoj.gov/ndic/pubs3/3690/marijuan.htm#Top]
[219] NDIC, *North Carolina Drug Threat Assessment*, April 2003.
[http://www.usdoj.gov/ndic/pubs3/3690/marijuan.htm#Top]
[220] NDIC, *North Carolina Drug Threat Assessment*, April 2003.
[http://www.usdoj.gov/ndic/pubs3/3690/marijuan.htm#Top]

authorities in North Carolina seized 801 kilograms of marijuana in 1998, 2,301 kilograms in 1999, 4,885 kilograms in 2000, and 3,826.8 kilograms in 2001, according to FDSS data.

Major Avenues into the State: Mexican trafficking organizations have been smuggling marijuana into the state, particularly into the central portion (Piedmont). The marijuana comes directly from Mexico by containerized cargo transported by tractor-trailer trucks. In addition, marijuana is being smuggled in ever-larger amounts by campers, pickup trucks, and larger vehicles.

Criminal groups, particularly Jamaican, also transport marijuana into North Carolina on commercial airlines, employing couriers who conceal the drug in their luggage or strap packages of it under their clothing. Mexican drug-trafficking organizations based in Mexico supply marijuana to Jamaican criminal groups in San Diego, California, who then distribute the drug to other Jamaican criminal groups in North Carolina and other southeastern states. Mexican, African-American, and Caucasian criminal groups also transport marijuana into North Carolina from southwestern states via package delivery services. Mexican, African American, and Caucasian criminal groups also transport marijuana into the state on buses and passenger trains.[221]

Links to Organized Crime: In North Carolina, Mexican criminal groups are the primary wholesale distributors of marijuana produced in Mexico. African American, Caucasian, and Jamaican criminal groups also distribute wholesale quantities of Mexico-produced marijuana.[222]

NORTH DAKOTA

Marijuana Situation: Marijuana is one of the primary drugs of choice in North Dakota and the most readily available illicit drug in the state. Marijuana availability is increasing throughout North Dakota.

Production: Marijuana is increasingly available from local cultivators. Local cultivation of marijuana, however, is relatively small scale. Ditch weed, initially grown for the hemp used to produce rope during World War II, is abundant in the southeastern part of North Dakota. In 2002 more than 3 million ditch-weed plants were eradicated.

---

[221] NDIC, *North Carolina Drug Threat Assessment*, April 2003.
[http://www.usdoj.gov/ndic/pubs3/3690/marijuan.htm#Top]
[222] NDIC, *North Carolina Drug Threat Assessment*, April 2003.

Indoor Domestic Grows: Most of the locally grown cannabis is cultivated indoors, accounting for an estimated 80 percent of all seizures in the state.[223]

Outdoor Domestic Grows: Less common than indoor grows.

Processed and Imported: Mexico-produced and, to a lesser extent, locally produced marijuana are the most common types available; however, Canada-produced marijuana also is available.[224]

Federal Drug (Marijuana) Seizures: 0.4 kilograms, 2002 (DEA). Marijuana seizures by North Dakota law enforcement officials nearly doubled, going from 258 pounds in 1993 to 507 pounds in 1999.[225]

Major Avenues into the State: The supplies emanate mainly from the Southwest Border. Private vehicles and commercial mail carriers are used to ship small quantities, ranging from five to ten pounds, while tractor-trailers are used to transport larger shipments. Mexican criminal groups transport most of the marijuana available in the state. These groups primarily use private vehicles to transport the drug from Mexico through the southwestern states into North Dakota. They also use Chicago, Denver, and Minneapolis as distribution centers and receive direct shipments of pound, multi-pound, and kilogram quantities from Laredo, Brownsville, and Crystal City, Texas. Marijuana also is transported into North Dakota from Manitoba, Canada.[226]

Links to Organized Crime: Mexico-based drug-trafficking organizations dominate and manage the transportation of marijuana from the Southwest Border to North Dakota. To transport the marijuana from the Southwest Border, these organizations utilize tractor-trailers, many of which have sophisticated traps installed.

OHIO

Marijuana Situation: Marijuana is the most widely abused and readily available illicit drug throughout the state of Ohio.

Production: Ohio is a source area for marijuana cultivation. Cannabis is cultivated throughout the state at both outdoor and indoor grow sites.[227]

---

[223] NDIC, *North Dakota Drug Threat Assessment*, May 2002.
[http://www.usdoj.gov/ndic/pubs1/1052/marijuan.htm#Top]
[224] NDIC, *North Dakota Drug Threat Assessment*, May 2002.
[225] NDIC, *North Dakota Drug Threat Assessment*, May 2002.
[226] NDIC, *North Dakota Drug Threat Assessment*, May 2002.
[227] NDIC, *Ohio Drug Threat Assessment Update*, July 2002.
[http://www.usdoj.gov/ndic/pubs1/1798/marijuan.htm#Top]

Indoor Domestic Grows: Indoor grows often are located in residential basements and have intricate lighting systems to stimulate plant growth. In northern Ohio, the use of hydroponics and other sophisticated indoor growing techniques that produce sinsemilla with a high THC content continues to increase.

Outdoor Domestic Grows: Outdoor grow sites are located on public and private land usually in remote areas. The rural areas of Ohio provide an adequate environment for the outdoor cultivation of cannabis, most of which occurs in the southern part of the state.

Processed and Imported: The available supply of marijuana ranges from one pound to multi-hundred pound quantities. Mexican marijuana is frequently encountered in the state of Ohio.

Federal Drug (Marijuana) Seizures, 2002: 775 kilograms.

Major Avenues into the State: Ohio is a distribution point for Mexican marijuana from the southwest border. Large quantities are shipped into Ohio mainly overland from the southwest border states, and smaller quantities through package delivery services and the mail.

Links to Organized Crime: Mexican criminal groups are the dominant wholesale suppliers of marijuana in Ohio. They supply multi-hundred kilogram quantities of marijuana to most districts throughout the state. Local independent and Jamaican criminal groups also are responsible for shipping and distributing wholesale amounts of marijuana into Ohio in multi-kilogram quantities.

OKLAHOMA

Marijuana Situation: Marijuana is readily available in all areas of Oklahoma and is the main illegal drug of abuse in the state.

Production: Domestically produced marijuana is available in Oklahoma, though not as readily in recent years. Oklahoma, along with several other southern states, has endured severe drought conditions over the past three years. This situation has affected the local production of marijuana.

The northeastern and southeastern regions of Oklahoma are major cannabis cultivation areas for high-quality marijuana. Growers continue to cultivate cannabis in the rugged, forested terrain of southeastern Oklahoma in areas such as the Ouachita National Forest, which is located along the Arkansas border. Within Oklahoma, cannabis grows usually consist of 100 or fewer plants and typically are located near a water source. In the rugged, remote areas of northeastern Oklahoma, cannabis is grown in individual plots consisting of 20 or fewer plants. Once harvested, this marijuana is distributed locally or, to a lesser extent, transported out of state. In the Oklahoma City and Tulsa areas, locally grown cannabis is in high demand due to its high quality and because local residents prefer to deal with known local suppliers.[228]

Indoor Domestic Grows: Cannabis eradication efforts by state officials as well as a recent drought have caused many outdoor growers to shift their operations to indoor grow locations. Hydroponics and aeroponics are just two types of cultivation methods that are currently used by local growers.[229]

Outdoor Domestic Grows: No information available.

Processed and Imported: Marijuana imported from Mexico is prevalent. Mexican "Sensimilla," usually found in "pressed/brick" form, is the most common type of marijuana seen in Oklahoma, particularly in urban areas.

Federal Drug (Marijuana) Seizures, 2002: 490.4 kilograms.

Major Avenues into the State: Marijuana imported from Mexico is usually imported in combination with other illegal drugs being transported to Oklahoma and other states north and east. The majority of the marijuana is imported from the southwest border by passenger vehicle and occasionally in freight vehicles.

Links to Organized Crime: Mexican drug-trafficking organizations and Mexican criminal groups are the primary wholesale distributors of Mexico-produced marijuana available in Oklahoma.[230]

OREGON

Marijuana Situation: Oregon is a source of marijuana, which is readily available in the state.

Production:

Indoor Domestic Grows: The majority of marijuana available in Portland is cultivated in home grow operations.

Outdoor Domestic Grows: No information available.

Processed and Imported: Canadian and domestic marijuana in the Portland area is available in multi-pound amounts. Mexican marijuana is present, but not prevalent.

Federal Drug (Marijuana) Seizures, 2002: 19.5 kilograms.

---

[228] NDIC, *Oklahoma Drug Threat Assessment*, October 2002.
[http://www.usdoj.gov/ndic/pubs2/2286/marijuan.htm#Top]
[229] NDIC, *Oklahoma Drug Threat Assessment*, October 2002.
[230] NDIC, *Oklahoma Drug Threat Assessment*, October 2002.

Major Avenues into the State: Mexican-grown marijuana is transported using existing heroin and methamphetamine distribution routes and methods. It is typically transported overland via Interstate 5 and U.S. Highway 101 in western Oregon. Traffickers typically use passenger vehicles fitted with hidden compartments or attempt to otherwise conceal the drugs within the vehicle. Canadian marijuana smugglers use passenger vehicles, fishing vessels, private aircraft (fixed wing and helicopters), and "mules" to smuggle the drug into the state. Traffickers take advantage of rural airfields to smuggle large quantities of marijuana.

Links to Organized Crime:

PENNSYLVANIA[231]

Marijuana Situation: Marijuana is the most widely available and commonly abused illicit drug in Pennsylvania. It is abundantly available in both wholesale and retail quantities in the state. In western Pennsylvania, marijuana abundance is attributed to the continued use of commercial shipping companies to transport it as well as the existence of growing operations in the area. Recreational use of marijuana is popular with high school- and college-age students, but adults are the predominant users of marijuana, especially in large social gatherings, such as rock concerts. Marijuana is typically smoked in combination with crack cocaine, heroin, and PCP.

Production: Significant quantities of locally produced marijuana are available. Cannabis is grown both outdoors and indoors in Pennsylvania. Caucasian criminal groups and local independent dealers are the primary cultivators of cannabis in the state.

Indoor Domestic Grows: Local indoor grows are still not common in the Philadelphia area, but they are increasing.[232]

Outdoor Domestic Grows: Most outdoor cultivation occurs in the northwestern part of the state, particularly in Erie, Crawford, Mercer, Venango, and Warren counties. Cannabis increasingly is cultivated in remote areas to avoid detection. Some growers are using private farmland, typically owned by others, or public lands to avoid property seizures and forfeitures.

Processed and Imported: Most of the marijuana available in the state is produced in Mexico, but marijuana produced in other states, as well as in Canada and Jamaica, is available.

---

[231] This section incorporates data from NDIC, *Pennsylvania Drug Threat Assessment Update*, October 2003. [http://www.usdoj.gov/ndic/pubs6/6180/marijuan.htm#Top]
[232] "Marijuana," *Pulse Check*: Trends in Drug Abuse, Office of National Drug Control Policy, November 2002. [http://www.whitehousedrugpolicy.gov/publications/drugfact/pulsechk/]

Federal Drug (Marijuana) Seizures, 2001-02: 28.6 kilograms. (DEA). According to FDSS data, federal law enforcement officials in Pennsylvania seized 1,567.5 kilograms of marijuana in 2002, a significant increase from the 377.3 kilograms seized in 2001.[233]

Major Avenues into the State: Marijuana is transported into the state primarily by private and commercial vehicles from Arizona, California, Texas, and Mexico, among other areas. It also is transported into the state by rental vehicles; by couriers aboard commercial aircraft, buses, and trains; by package delivery services; and occasionally by maritime vessels. Because of their proximity to major thoroughfares, localities throughout the state are transshipment points as well as consumer markets. In particular, the city of Reading and areas in central Pennsylvania, which are homes to several trucking warehouses, serve as hubs for marijuana trafficking organizations transporting bulk loads of marijuana to distributors in the eastern United States. In general, Philadelphia's street corner distribution networks are the main sources of supply for drugs sold to users throughout the state.

Links to Organized Crime: Jamaican and Mexican criminal groups are the primary wholesale-level marijuana transporters of marijuana into Pennsylvania and distributors in the state. Most trafficking and distribution is perpetrated by a variety of Hispanic and African-American organizations that are scattered throughout Pennsylvania and Delaware. Some of these groups are connected primarily to sources in New York City, yet some distribute drugs that were either brought to the region via other transshipment locations or that were shipped or transported directly to Philadelphia or other localities from source areas. At the retail level, Hispanic, African-American, and Caucasian groups, along with some dominant Jamaican organizations, control the marijuana market by distributing bag, ounce, and pound quantities to users across Pennsylvania and Delaware.

RHODE ISLAND

Marijuana Situation: Marijuana is the most widely available and commonly abused illicit drug in Rhode Island. The marijuana trend in Rhode Island supports a widespread and readily available market of fairly large amounts of this drug. Prices of marijuana will vary seasonally as the supply fluctuates. The marijuana available in Rhode Island is mostly Mexican; however it is

---

[233] NDIC, *Pennsylvania Drug Threat Assessment Update*, October 2003.

supplemented by limited amounts of other foreign based and domestic marijuana.
Hydroponically produced marijuana is also available in Rhode Island.

Production: Some of the marijuana available in Rhode Island is produced within the state.

Indoor Domestic Grows: Cannabis is cultivated primarily indoors in Rhode Island.

Outdoor Domestic Grows: There is some outdoor cultivation in the state.

Processed and Imported: Most of the marijuana available in Rhode Island is produced in
Mexico; marijuana produced in Canada and Jamaica also is available.[234]

Federal Drug (Marijuana) Seizures: 0.6 kilograms, 2002 (DEA). The amount of marijuana
seized by federal law enforcement officials in Rhode Island fluctuated from 1998 through 2002.
According to FDSS data, federal law enforcement officials in Rhode Island seized 160.5
kilograms of marijuana in 1998, 2.6 kilograms in 1999, 1.3 kilograms in 2000, 8.5 kilograms in
2001, and 90.4 kilograms in 2002.[235]

Major Avenues into the State: Marijuana from foreign and domestic sources is transported into
Rhode Island by various groups using a variety of methods, including parcel carriers and couriers
on commercial airlines. Mexican criminal groups transport multi-kilogram shipments of
marijuana from sources in Mexico and transportation hubs in California and southwestern states,
primarily using commercial and private vehicles. Marijuana transported in commercial vehicles
often is intermingled with legitimate cargo, and marijuana transported in private vehicles often is
concealed in hidden compartments. Caucasian, Dominican, and Jamaican criminal groups as well
as various local independent dealers also transport marijuana into Rhode Island. A majority of
the "hydro" marijuana is transported into Rhode Island by tractor-trailers. Canada is the major
source of supply for this type of marijuana in Rhode Island.[236]

Since September 11, 2001, Dominican criminal groups have altered their methods of
transportation when smuggling marijuana into Rhode Island. Prior to September 11, members of
Dominican criminal groups would fly to southwestern states, purchase marijuana from Mexican
suppliers, and then transport the drug back to Rhode Island concealed in luggage. Although some

---

[234] NDIC, *Rhode Island Drug Threat Assessment Update*, July 2002.
[http://www.usdoj.gov/ndic/pubs3/3979/marijuan.htm#Top]
[235] NDIC, *Rhode Island Drug Threat Assessment Update*, July 2002.
[236] This paragraph is largely based on NDIC, *Rhode Island Drug Threat Assessment Update*, July 2002.

members of such groups continue to transport marijuana as couriers aboard commercial aircraft, they more frequently use package delivery services.[237]

Links to Organized Crime: Mexican criminal groups are the primary transporters of marijuana into Rhode Island. However, Dominican criminal groups are also involved.

SOUTH CAROLINA

Marijuana Situation: Marijuana is the most prevalent illegal drug of abuse in South Carolina.

Production: Outdoor cannabis fields are more common than indoor operations in South Carolina, but indoor operations are increasing significantly. Local independent dealers, mostly Caucasian, are the primary growers of cannabis, operating mostly in the rural areas of the state. The sparsely populated regions of South Carolina that have adequate precipitation provide an environment conducive to the domestic cultivation of cannabis.[238]

Indoor Domestic Grows: Less common than outdoor grows.

Outdoor Domestic Grows: Many cannabis growers concerned with mandatory sentencing requirements for cultivating large single plots have begun planting numerous smaller plots containing fewer plants scattered over a larger area. Many growers attempt elaborate concealment methods to disguise cannabis plants from law enforcement detection. Members of the South Carolina National Guard and the South Carolina Law Enforcement Division (SLED) routinely eradicate small patches of outdoor marijuana.

Processed and Imported: Mexico is the most common source location. Being less expensive, Mexico-produced marijuana is more widely available than locally produced marijuana and is transported into the state in large quantities.[239]

Federal Drug (Marijuana) Seizures, 2002: 544.8 kilograms.

Major Avenues into the State: Mexican criminal groups are the primary transporters of marijuana into the state. Multi-kilogram shipments of marijuana also are transported to South Carolina from the Southwest Border area, Florida, and Georgia. Multi-hundred-kilogram shipments of marijuana have been occasionally transshipped through the Port of Charleston. Mexican criminal groups smuggle marijuana into South Carolina from Mexico through the

---

[237] NDIC, *Rhode Island Drug Threat Assessment Update*, July 2002, citing the DEA Providence Resident Office.
[238] NDIC, *South Carolina Drug Threat Assessment Update*, December 2001.
[http://www.usdoj.gov/ndic/pubs07/717/marijuan.htm#Top]
[239] NDIC, *South Carolina Drug Threat Assessment Update*, December 2001.

Southwest Border area, using the interstate highway system, mostly in private vehicles. Interstate 40 is a major transit route for Mexico-produced marijuana destined for South Carolina. Local distributors also transport Mexico-produced and Caribbean-produced marijuana into South Carolina from Atlanta via interstates 85 and 20, and from Florida via the I-95 corridor. [240]

Distributors also use parcel delivery services and commercial tractor-trailers, airlines, buses, trains, and ships to transport marijuana into the state. Distributors frequently mail multi-kilogram shipments of marijuana to South Carolina from California and Texas. Multi-kilogram quantities of marijuana also have been seized from airline passengers traveling to South Carolina from Los Angeles, Houston, and Las Vegas and from commercial bus passengers traveling from Mexico, Florida, and Texas to the state. Maritime vessels also are used to smuggle multi-hundred-kilogram quantities of marijuana directly from Mexico and the Caribbean through the Port of Charleston to the eastern United States.[241] Traffickers utilize 40-foot and 20-foot shipping containers to transport contraband, which is secreted in the midst of legitimate commercial products.

South Carolina is identified more as a drug "consumer state" rather than as a "source state." However, there has been increasing evidence of organizational activity extending to major distribution hubs. In the case of marijuana, these hubs include southern Texas/Mexico and southern California. Additionally, Mexican-based traffickers have taken advantage of the increase in Latino immigration to the state by hiding within Hispanic enclaves.

Links to Organized Crime: Mexican criminal groups, outlaw motorcycle gangs, and Caucasian and African-American independent dealers control wholesale distribution of marijuana in South Carolina.[242] In addition to targeting Mexican drug-trafficking organizations, recent investigations have targeted Cuban, Haitian, and Jamaican traffickers.

SOUTH DAKOTA

Marijuana Situation: Marijuana is readily available in all areas of South Dakota. It is the most abused of the illegal controlled substances.

Production:

---

[240] NDIC, *South Carolina Drug Threat Assessment Update*, December 2001.
[241] NDIC, *South Carolina Drug Threat Assessment Update*, December 2001.
[242] NDIC, *South Carolina Drug Threat Assessment Update*, December 2001.

Indoor Domestic Grows: Higher-purity marijuana is produced in indoor grow operations, which typically contain fewer than 100 plants, in the Sioux Falls area. Larger indoor operations have been found in the Rapid City area in western South Dakota, ranging from a few plants to several hundred.

Outdoor Domestic Grows: The controversial issue of "hemp" is a high-profile topic. During 2001-02, members of the Oglala Sioux Tribe attempted to plant fields of "hemp" on the Pine Ridge Indian Reservation in South Dakota.

Processed and Imported: Marijuana imported from Mexico is common.

Federal Drug (Marijuana) Seizures, 2002: 1.7 kilograms.

Major Avenues into the State: Multi-hundred-pound quantities of marijuana are transported into the state from the southwest border of the United States. Smaller quantities are also shipped by express mail services or purchased from Hispanic males in the Sioux City area and driven back to Sioux Falls. Trafficking organizations are increasingly using Interstate 90, which runs east to west through South Dakota, for the transportation of drugs and currency.

Links to Organized Crime: No information available.

TENNESSEE

Marijuana Situation: Marijuana is the most readily available drug in Tennessee. Marijuana abuse and trafficking is a serious problem throughout the state and especially in rural areas. Marijuana is favored over other drugs of abuse by some in certain areas of Tennessee, which is predominantly a "user" and a transshipment state. Tennessee is not a major source area for any drug except domestically grown marijuana.

Production: Tennessee is a major supplier of domestically grown marijuana. Tennessee, along with West Virginia and Kentucky, produces the majority of the United States' supply of domestic marijuana. Prosecution of marijuana growers in the state has been extremely difficult because of a gap in intelligence on crop locations and because many of the domestic marijuana sites detected are so small that even if the owner/grower were identified, the U.S. Attorney would be reluctant to prosecute.

Indoor Domestic Grows: Indoor cannabis grows are becoming more common in Tennessee. Indoor cannabis cultivators using hydroponic techniques produce marijuana with higher levels of

THC. Indoor cannabis production, which occurs year-round, is easily concealed from law enforcement officials and thieves.[243]

Outdoor Domestic Grows: Cannabis is cultivated primarily outdoors in Tennessee, where growing conditions are ideal. Cannabis plants are cultivated primarily in the Appalachia-Cumberland Plateau region in eastern and central Tennessee, which has ample rainfall and a temperate climate. Between 1993 and 2000, Tennessee ranked among the top five states in the nation based on the number of cannabis plants eradicated. The quantity of cannabis eradicated in Tennessee in 1999 had an estimated street value of more than $628 million, surpassing the value of tobacco, the largest legitimate cash crop, which was valued at $218 million.

Processed and Imported: Mexico-produced marijuana is the type most commonly available in Tennessee. Mexican marijuana has also been seized in the state.

Federal Drug (Marijuana) Seizures: 19.4 kilograms, 2002 (DEA). According to FDSS data, federal law enforcement officials in Tennessee seized 2,120.4 kilograms of marijuana in 1999 and 3,015.7 kilograms in 2000. The Tennessee Bureau of Investigation seized 5.2 kilograms of marijuana in 1999 and 12.3 kilograms in 2000. "Law enforcement officials" seized 199.8 kilograms of marijuana in 1999 and 148.1 kilograms in 2000 under Operation Jetway and 2,395.4 kilograms of marijuana in 1999 and 5,658.3 kilograms in 2000 under Operation Pipeline.

Major Avenues into the State: Geographically, Tennessee is unique because it is bordered by eight other states. The interstate and state highway systems crisscross Tennessee's four major cities and traverse each of its borders. These highways, which carry a very large volume of traffic, are a primary means of moving drugs to and through Tennessee. As a result, the drug situations in the neighboring states have an impact on the drug situation in Tennessee.

Mexican criminal groups, some associated with Mexican drug-trafficking organizations, transport large quantities of marijuana into and through Tennessee in tractor-trailers from distribution centers primarily in Mexico, Arizona, California, and Texas. Mexican criminal groups usually transport between 100 and 1,000 pounds of marijuana per shipment. Mexico-produced marijuana also is transported into and through the state in private vehicles, especially large automobiles or sport utility vehicles with built-in concealed compartments in the gas tanks. African-American and Hispanic street gang members travel in private vehicles from Tennessee

---

[243] NDIC, *Tennessee Drug Threat Assessment Update*, May 2002.
[http://www.usdoj.gov/ndic/pubs1/1017/marijuan.htm#Top]

primarily to California, Florida, Illinois, Missouri, New York, and Texas to purchase Mexico-produced marijuana from other street gangs and transport the drug back. Members of Gangster Disciples and Vice Lords in western Tennessee commonly transport marijuana in private vehicles from Chicago and St. Louis to Tennessee on I-55. Members of Mara Salvatrucha in Nashville transport marijuana in private vehicles primarily from California, Texas, and New York via I-40 and I-81. Members of Niggas from Lonsdale, a Knoxville-based gang, transport marijuana in private vehicles from Florida using I-75 and New York using I-81. Mexican criminal groups also ship Mexico-produced marijuana into and through Tennessee concealed in packages sent through commercial package delivery services.[244]

Links to Organized Crime: Mexican criminal groups and, to a lesser extent, street gangs such as Gangster Disciples, Mara Salvatrucha, and Vice Lords are the primary wholesale distributors of Mexico-produced marijuana in Tennessee.[245]

TEXAS

Marijuana Situation: Marijuana is readily available and is considered the most widely used illegal drug throughout the State of Texas. Largely because of its multifaceted transportation infrastructure and its proximity to Mexico and other Latin American production countries, Texas is a national distribution center for illicit drugs.

Production: Marijuana produced in Texas is available, although to a lesser extent than marijuana produced in Mexico.[246] Cannabis is cultivated in the state at indoor and outdoor grow sites. Caucasian criminal groups and independent Caucasian producers are the primary cultivators of cannabis within Texas. Mexican criminal groups and independent Mexican producers also cultivate cannabis in the state, but to a lesser extent.[247]

Indoor Domestic Grows: Indoor grow sites are located in every part of the state. In recent years, increased enforcement activity has led to the seizure of several significant indoor marijuana cultivation operations in the North Texas area. These operations range in size from 100 to more than 1,100 plants and have produced marijuana with THC levels as high as 15 percent.

---

[244] NDIC, *Tennessee Drug Threat Assessment Update*, May 2002, citing the DEA Memphis Resident Office.
[245] NDIC, *Tennessee Drug Threat Assessment Update*, May 2002.
[246] NDIC, *Texas Drug Threat Assessment*, Document ID: 2003-S0387TX-001, October 2003.
[http://www.usdoj.gov/ndic/pubs5/5624/index.htm]
[247] NDIC, *Texas Drug Threat Assessment*, October 2003.

Outdoor Domestic Grows: Outdoor grow sites primarily are located in the eastern and northern areas of the state. The climate and topography in western and southern Texas are not conducive to outdoor cannabis cultivation. Cannabis cultivators often use dense, forested areas as cultivation sites to avoid detection by law enforcement. These cultivation sites are typically small, containing 30 to 40 plants, well concealed, and scattered over large areas.[248]

Processed and Imported: Marijuana produced in Mexico is the predominant type available and trafficked in the state.[249]

Federal Drug (Marijuana) Seizures, 2002: 136,870.8 kilograms. NDIC reports 555,324 kilograms.[250]

Earlier Federal Drug (Marijuana) Seizures: Marijuana frequently is seized in Texas, and seizures often involve large quantities of the drug. FDSS statistics, which are higher than those in Table 11, indicate that the quantity of marijuana seized by federal law enforcement officers in Texas increased dramatically from 364,525 kilograms in 1998 to 540,197 in 1999, 610,828 kilograms in 2000, and 555,324 in 2002.[251] State and local law enforcement officers in Texas reporting to Operations Pipeline/Convoy seized a total of 63,514 kilograms of marijuana from commercial and private vehicles traveling on Texas highways in 2000. Marijuana was, by far, the most frequently seized drug under Operations Pipeline/Convoy.[252]

Major Avenues into the State: Texas is a significant entry point for marijuana smuggled into the United States. The EPIC (El Paso Intelligence Center) data reflecting drug seizures made within 150 miles of the U.S.-Mexico border indicate that more marijuana was seized in Texas than in any other state along the border from 1999 through 2002.[253]

Marijuana is imported primarily from the Texas/Mexico border by privately owned vehicles and commercial trucks. The U.S. Border Patrol often makes multi-hundred-pound marijuana seizures from "backpackers" at points along the Rio Grande River, and from vehicles transiting at the U.S. Border Patrol secondary checkpoints located inside Texas. At the Ports of Entry, ton-quantity seizures of marijuana are often made from commercial trucks attempting to

---

[248] NDIC, *Texas Drug Threat Assessment*, October 2003.
[249] NDIC, *Texas Drug Threat Assessment*, October 2003.
[250] NDIC, *Texas Drug Threat Assessment*, October 2003.
[251] NDIC, *Texas Drug Threat Assessment*, October 2003.
[252] NDIC, *Texas Drug Threat Assessment*, October 2003.
[253] NDIC, *Texas Drug Threat Assessment*, October 2003.

enter the United States. Large quantities of marijuana are routinely seized by all levels of law enforcement during highway interdiction stops in the North Texas area.[254]

Marijuana transporters also smuggle marijuana into Texas using couriers traveling aboard commercial and private aircraft, buses, boats, and passenger trains; couriers traveling between points of entry on horses, all-terrain vehicles, and foot; and package delivery services.[255] In addition, Mexican drug-trafficking organizations also smuggle marijuana into the state by coastal freighters and fishing boats.[256] Yet another means of transport used by drug transporters to smuggle marijuana into Texas are freight railcars.[257]

The greater Dallas/Fort Worth area serves primarily as a drug distribution and transshipment area. The area's central location and its physical and cultural proximity to the Mexican Border provide a natural advantage for drug distribution/transshipment. As a result of its geographical location and extensive transportation infrastructure, Houston continues to be a primary transshipment area for the bulk importation of most major categories of drugs, including marijuana. As a result of the North American Free Trade Agreement (NAFTA), the El Paso/Ciudad Juárez area has experienced a significant increase in cross-border traffic in recent years. The people crossing the international bridges on a daily basis and the large transportation industry available in this area (air, bus, trucking, and rail) provide drug traffickers with innumerable drug and money-smuggling opportunities. Rural, desert-like areas in New Mexico and West Texas, whether they be large ranches or National Park land backing up to the border, or some easily crossed places along the Rio Grande, offer plentiful smuggling opportunities to drug-trafficking organizations. The Southwest Border area of Texas is largely rural and sparsely populated and includes the Big Bend Corridor, a transshipment route for drugs entering the United States from Northeast Mexico en route to Midland/Odessa and other cities in the United States.

Links to Organized Crime: Mexican drug-trafficking organizations dominate the smuggling of marijuana from Mexico into Texas. They typically smuggle marijuana into Texas across the U.S.-Mexico border through points of entry and transport the drug to locations within the state or

---

[254] NDIC, *Texas Drug Threat Assessment*, October 2003.
[255] NDIC, *Texas Drug Threat Assessment*, October 2003.
[256] NDIC, *Texas Drug Threat Assessment*, October 2003.
[257] NDIC, *Texas Drug Threat Assessment*, October 2003.

to drug markets throughout the country.[258] Drug smuggling and transportation in the Dallas/Fort Worth area are dominated by major Mexican drug-trafficking organizations. These groups are polydrug organizations smuggling marijuana and other illegal drugs to the Dallas/Fort Worth area for distribution in the Eastern, Southeastern, and Midwestern United States. Drug smuggling and illicit transportation in the Houston area are primarily dominated by Mexican, Colombian, and Dominican polydrug-trafficking organizations.

UTAH

Marijuana Situation: Marijuana is a popular drug in Utah and is the most widely available illicit drug in the state.

Production: Although most of the marijuana available in Utah is produced in Mexico and California, cannabis is cultivated in the state, particularly in the northern areas.

Indoor Domestic Grows: Significant quantities are produced indoors. Caucasian criminal groups and local independent dealers dominate the production of high-potency marijuana at indoor grow sites throughout Utah.[259] Homemade irrigation systems have been developed to counteract the arid climate of these remote sites and camouflage techniques have become more sophisticated.

Outdoor Domestic Grows: Outdoor cultivation is the more common method of producing marijuana in Utah. Cannabis is easily grown in the remote areas of the state, which are most conducive for growing operations due to the fertile soil. Some owners of outdoor grows have utilized armed Mexican immigrants to tend the plants. Weber County is the center of cannabis cultivation in the state. Mexican criminal groups and, to a lesser extent, Caucasian local independent dealers, increasingly are using public lands in Utah for cannabis cultivation.[260]

Processed and Imported: Marijuana produced by Mexican criminal groups in Mexico and California is the most common type available in the state. Generally, marijuana produced in Mexico and California has a lower potency than locally produced marijuana and sells for a lower price at the wholesale level.[261] The importation of marijuana from British Columbia, Canada, remains active in Utah.

---

[258] NDIC, *Texas Drug Threat Assessment*, October 2003.
[259] NDIC, *Utah Drug Threat Assessment*, March 2003.
[260] NDIC, *Utah Drug Threat Assessment*, March 2003.
[261] NDIC, *Utah Drug Threat Assessment*, March 2003.

Federal Drug (Marijuana) Seizures: 1.5 kilograms, 2002 (DEA). According to FDSS data, marijuana seizures made by federal law enforcement officers in Utah decreased from 635 kilograms in 1998 to 13 kilograms in 2001. Law enforcement officials in Utah reported marijuana seizures totaling 950 kilograms in 1999, 437 kilograms in 2000, and 490 kilograms in 2001 as part of Operation Pipeline. They did not report any marijuana seizures in 2000 as part of Operation Jetway; however, in 2001 they reported seizing 14 kilograms of the drug.[262]

Major Avenues into the State: Mexican criminal groups dominate the transportation of marijuana into Utah. These criminal groups transport marijuana primarily from Mexico. Some Caucasian and Mexican local independent dealers as well as street gangs also transport marijuana from transshipment points in California, Colorado, and Nevada into the state. Caucasian criminal groups and local independent dealers are the primary transporters of high-potency marijuana into and throughout Utah from Colorado, Oregon, Washington, and British Columbia, Canada. Marijuana typically is transported into Utah in private or rental vehicles via interstate 15, 70, and 80 and US 89 and US 191. Commercial and private aircraft, buses, and package delivery services also are used.[263] Most of the marijuana transported into Utah, often in wholesale quantities, is in transit to other areas of the United States. Transportation routes for marijuana transiting Utah include interstates 15 and 70 and US 191.[264]

Links to Organized Crime: In Utah, Mexican criminal groups are the predominant wholesale and mid-level distributors of marijuana produced by Mexican criminal groups in Mexico and California.[265]

VERMONT

Marijuana Situation: Marijuana, which is readily available in all areas of the state, is the most widely abused and readily available drug in Vermont.

Production: Cannabis is cultivated both outdoors and indoors throughout Vermont.

Indoor Domestic Grows: Indoor grows, to include hydroponic systems, are maintained on a small scale.

---

[262] NDIC, *Utah Drug Threat Assessment*, March 2003.
[263] NDIC, *Utah Drug Threat Assessment*, March 2003.
[264] NDIC, *Utah Drug Threat Assessment*, March 2003.
[265] NDIC, *Utah Drug Threat Assessment*, March 2003.

Outdoor Domestic Grows: In the past, local growers maintained large-scale outdoor cultivation operations. However, the current trend of local marijuana cultivation has changed to small outdoor plots that can be difficult to detect.

Processed and Imported: Most of the marijuana available in Vermont is produced in Mexico; however, high-quality BC Bud from Canada and locally produced marijuana also are available.[266] Mexican and hydroponically grown marijuana from Canada are common in the state.

Federal Drug (Marijuana) Seizures: 16.6 kilograms, 2002 (DEA). According to FDSS data, federal law enforcement officials seized 450.1 kilograms of marijuana in 2002.[267]

Major Avenues into the State: Various criminal groups, street gangs, and local independent dealers transport marijuana into Vermont. Most of the Mexico-produced marijuana available in the state is transported from Massachusetts and New York in private or rental vehicles. However, package delivery services and couriers aboard commercial aircraft also are used to transport marijuana into the state, often directly from areas near the U.S.-Mexico border. Higher-quality, Canada-produced marijuana also is smuggled across the U.S.-Canada border using similar conveyances; couriers go on foot or use snowmobiles or all-terrain vehicles. Vermont's two interstate highways 89 and 91 terminate at the U.S./Canada border, providing drug traffickers easy access to metropolitan areas in Canada and the United States. Once across the border, marijuana smugglers typically rendezvous with individuals who then transport the drug via private vehicle to locations throughout Vermont or on to Massachusetts, New York, and other states. Canada-produced marijuana occasionally is smuggled across the U.S.-Canada border into Vermont by Hells Angels outlaw motorcycle gang members, primarily in private vehicles.[268]

Links to Organized Crime: Loosely organized Caucasian criminal groups and Caucasian local independent dealers are the primary retail-level marijuana distributors in the state.[269]

---

[266] NDIC, *Utah Drug Threat Assessment*, March 2003.
[267] NDIC, *Vermont Drug Threat Assessment Update*, May 2002.
[http://www.usdoj.gov/ndic/pubs3/3999/marijuan.htm#Top]
[268] NDIC, *Vermont Drug Threat Assessment Update*, May 2002.
[269] NDIC, *Vermont Drug Threat Assessment Update*, May 2002

VIRGINIA

Marijuana Situation: Marijuana is the most widely abused and most readily available drug in the state of Virginia.

Production: Cannabis cultivation in Virginia is widespread.

Indoor Domestic Grows: Indoor grows are increasingly common. Hydroponic indoor grows have not been encountered.

Outdoor Domestic Grows: Outdoor marijuana cultivation flourishes during the spring and summer.

Processed and Imported: Most of the marijuana available in the state is commercial grade product, imported from the southwestern United States. Demand for high-grade marijuana, however, is at extremely high levels, with source areas ranging from the Pacific Northwest to the New England states.

Federal Drug (Marijuana) Seizures, 2002: 27.5 kilograms.

Major Avenues into the State: Most of the marijuana available in Virginia is transported from southwestern states. Jamaican criminal groups are the primary transporters of marijuana into the state. Mexican criminal groups based in North Carolina also transport marijuana into Virginia, most frequently to the central and western parts of the state. Marijuana typically is transported via private vehicles and package delivery services. Additional quantities of marijuana are transported into the state via commercial vehicles and couriers aboard commercial aircraft, buses, and trains.[270] Virginia cities situated along Interstate 95 are vulnerable to "spillover" drug distribution from traffickers moving between the two major eastern drug importation hubs of New York City and Miami.

Links to Organized Crime: Local independent dealers and criminal groups, primarily Jamaicans and Mexicans, are the principal wholesale- and retail-level marijuana distributors in Virginia.[271] Mexican trafficking organizations are making enormous inroads in the marijuana distribution markets in nearly every part of the state.

---

[270] NDIC, *Virginia Drug Threat Assessment Update*, June 2003.
[http://www.usdoj.gov/ndic/pubs4/4531/marijuan.htm#Top]
[271] NDIC, *Virginia Drug Threat Assessment Update*, June 2003.

WASHINGTON

Marijuana Situation: Marijuana is readily available in multi-pound quantities throughout the state. Three types are normally encountered: locally grown (either from indoor or outdoor grow operations), Canadian BC Bud, and Mexican marijuana. Of these varieties, locally grown sinsemilla and BC Bud are preferred, because they have a far superior THC content than Mexican grown marijuana. Canadian BC Bud is the most prevalent variety in many areas, given the proximity to the border and the extent of cross border smuggling.

Production: Cannabis cultivation occurs throughout the state and may be increasing. Locally produced marijuana is the predominant type available throughout the state.[272]

Indoor Domestic Grows: Common.

Outdoor Domestic Grows: A large percentage of the cannabis cultivation in Washington occurs in the western portion of the state. Cannabis cultivators often use public lands such as national forests and parks, many of which are in the western part of the state, as cannabis cultivation sites because of their remote locations.[273]

Processed and Imported: The two main varieties of marijuana produced in Canada and Mexico are imported. Canada-produced marijuana (BC Bud) is more readily available in Washington than Mexico-produced marijuana.[274]

Federal Drug (Marijuana) Seizures: 103.6 kilograms, 2002 (DEA). According to FDSS data, federal law enforcement officials in Washington seized 1,193 kilograms of marijuana in 1998, 1,477 kilograms in 1999, 3,304 kilograms in 2000, and 4,164 kilograms in 2001.[275]

Major Avenues into the State: Sharing a border with Canada, Washington is a transshipment point for drugs entering Canada and Canadian marijuana (BC Bud), and other drugs entering the United States. Canada-based Asian criminal groups, primarily Vietnamese, and outlaw motorcycle gangs, primarily Hells Angels, as well as Caucasian criminal groups and local independent dealers based in Canada and Washington transport significant quantities of Canada-produced marijuana into the state. Canada-based Indian and Pakistani criminal groups also smuggle wholesale quantities of marijuana into the state, but to a lesser extent. Marijuana

---

[272] NDIC, *Washington Drug Threat Assessment Update*, February 2003.
[http://www.usdoj.gov/ndic/pubs3/3138/marijuan.htm#Top]
[273] NDIC, *Washington Drug Threat Assessment Update*, February 2003.
[274] NDIC, *Washington Drug Threat Assessment Update*, February 2003.
[275] NDIC, *Washington Drug Threat Assessment Update*, February 2003.

produced in Canada also is smuggled through Washington, primarily Seattle, en route to drug markets in surrounding states.[276]

Transporters use a variety of means to smuggle Canada-produced marijuana into Washington. They commonly smuggle Canada-produced marijuana into the state by private vehicle on I-5, on National Forest System roads, and on logging roads. Aircraft, all-terrain vehicles, boats, commercial buses, cold drops, commercial trucks, package delivery services, horses, kayaks, couriers with backpacks, and snowmobiles also are used.[277]

Marijuana produced in Mexico also is transported into Washington, but to a lesser extent than marijuana produced in Canada. Mexican criminal groups—often based in the Seattle-Tacoma area—are the dominant transporters of Mexico-produced marijuana into Washington. These criminal groups often transport Mexico-produced marijuana into the state by private vehicle on I-5 and US 97 and US 101.[278]

Links to Organized Crime: Mexican National polydrug organizations dominate the drug trade. However, various criminal groups, local independent dealers, and outlaw motorcycle gangs conduct wholesale marijuana distribution in Washington.[279]

WEST VIRGINIA

Marijuana Situation: Marijuana is the most widely available and commonly abused illicit drug in West Virginia.[280]

Production: West Virginia commonly serves as a source area for domestic marijuana. A substantial amount of the marijuana available in West Virginia is produced locally. Cannabis cultivation is common throughout the state, particularly in the southern counties of Boone, Cabell, Fayette, Lincoln, Logan, Mason, McDowell, Mingo, and Wayne. Caucasian local independent dealers and loosely organized criminal groups, composed primarily of family members and close friends, are the primary cannabis cultivators in West Virginia. Locally cultivated cannabis usually is harvested in August. Much of the marijuana produced is sold to local distributors and abusers as well as distributors in other states. The supply of locally

---

[276] NDIC, *Washington Drug Threat Assessment Update*, February 2003.
[277] NDIC, *Washington Drug Threat Assessment Update*, February 2003.
[278] NDIC, *Washington Drug Threat Assessment Update*, February 2003.
[279] NDIC, *Washington Drug Threat Assessment Update*, February 2003.
[280] NDIC, *West Virginia Drug Threat Assessment*, Document ID: 2003-S0379WV-001, August 2003.

produced marijuana typically is depleted by December, creating a demand for marijuana from other sources.[281]

Indoor Domestic Grows: Less common than outdoor grows.

Outdoor Domestic Grows: Most cannabis cultivators use land in rural and mountainous areas. They typically use public land or land owned by other people to avoid property seizures and forfeitures. Outdoor cannabis grows are more common than indoor grows in West Virginia (see Table 16). The DEA West Virginia domestic marijuana coordinator estimates that roughly 10 percent or less of the cannabis cultivated in West Virginia is eradicated each year.

Table 16. Cannabis Plots and Grows Seized and Plants Eradicated, West Virginia, 1998-2002					
	Year				
	1998	1999	2000	2001	2002
Outdoor plots seized	649	812	664	564	688
Outdoor plants eradicated	40,149	35,342	37,575	35,287	30,166
Indoor grows seized	24	41	53	30	39
Indoor plants eradicated	549	1,649	1,529	848	721
Source: DEA Domestic Cannabis Eradication/Suppression Program.					

Cultivators are now dispersing their plants over a larger area, sometimes using up to 300 separate plots, each containing one to four plants. This tactic makes detection by air, as well as eradication, more difficult for law enforcement.[282]

Processed and Imported: Most of the marijuana available in West Virginia is produced in Mexico, but a substantial amount is imported from neighboring states by Caucasian local independent dealers and loosely organized criminal groups that are composed primarily of family members and close friends.[283]

Federal Drug (marijuana) Seizures, 2002: 7.3 kilograms.

Earlier Federal Drug (marijuana) Seizures, 1998-2001: The amount of marijuana seized by federal law enforcement officials in West Virginia increased each year from 1998 through 2001,

---

[281] NDIC, *West Virginia Drug Threat Assessment*, August 2003.
[282] NDIC, *West Virginia Drug Threat Assessment*, August 2003.
[283] NDIC, *West Virginia Drug Threat Assessment*, August 2003.

before decreasing dramatically in 2002. According to FDSS data, federal law enforcement officials in West Virginia seized 4.1 kilograms of marijuana in 1998, 15.2 kilograms in 1999, 46.8 kilograms in 2000, 90.5 kilograms in 2001, and 7.3 kilograms in 2002.[284]

Major Avenues into the State: Drug distributors in West Virginia are uniquely placed to take advantage of sources of supply from both nearby eastern cities like Baltimore, Pittsburgh, or Washington, D.C., as well as large mid-western cities such as Columbus, Ohio; and Detroit, Michigan. In addition to receiving supplies from surrounding states, these dealers, groups, and gangs transport marijuana from southwestern states and Florida to West Virginia. They primarily use private vehicles and, to a lesser extent, commercial vehicles and package delivery services. Out-of-state transporters primarily use private vehicles equipped with hidden compartments, commercial vehicles, and couriers aboard buses and trains to transport marijuana to West Virginia. Transporters often package marijuana with dryer sheets, yellow mustard seeds, coffee grounds, jalapeño peppers, hot pepper flakes, cleaning products, or other materials to mask the drug's odor. Caucasian local independent dealers and loosely organized criminal groups routinely transport locally produced marijuana from West Virginia to surrounding states such as Ohio and Maryland, and as far south as Florida. These dealers and criminal groups primarily use private vehicles to transport West Virginia-produced marijuana to out-of-state locations.[285]

Links to Organized Crime: Caucasian and African-American local independent dealers and loosely organized criminal groups, composed primarily of family members and friends, are the principal transporters and wholesale- and retail-level distributors of most illicit drugs available in West Virginia.[286]

WISCONSIN

Marijuana Situation: Marijuana is the most readily available and most widely abused drug throughout Wisconsin. Sixty percent of prison inmates test positive for marijuana when entering correctional institutions, and one-fourth of all marijuana users also use other drugs.

Production: The availability of marijuana in the state is augmented by local cultivation. Cannabis is cultivated outdoors and indoors throughout Wisconsin. Violence associated with

---

[284] NDIC, *West Virginia Drug Threat Assessment*, August 2003.
[285] NDIC, *West Virginia Drug Threat Assessment*, August 2003.
[286] NDIC, *West Virginia Drug Threat Assessment*, August 2003.

cannabis cultivation is an increasing concern to Wisconsin law enforcement officers. Cannabis cultivators often are heavily armed and use boobytraps and warning devices to protect cultivation sites from law enforcement authorities and the public.

Indoor Domestic Grows: Indoor grows often are located in private residences. Wisconsin ranked fifth among all states for indoor marijuana growing activity in 2000, with 137 indoor grow sites seized.[287]

Outdoor Domestic Grows: Outdoor grow sites typically are located in remote areas on private land as well as public land.

Processed and Imported: Marijuana produced in Mexico is the dominant type.

Federal Drug (Marijuana) Seizures, 2002: 8 kilograms.

Major Avenues into the State: Mexican drug-trafficking organizations and criminal groups are the primary transporters of Mexico-produced marijuana into the state. These drug-trafficking organizations and criminal groups use private and rental vehicles, as well as tractor-trailers to transport bulk quantities of marijuana into Wisconsin from Mexico through southwestern states. Couriers on commercial aircraft also have been used to transport bulk quantities of marijuana into Wisconsin.[288] Milwaukee and Madison are both major destinations for Mexico-produced marijuana and transshipment points to other areas in the state.

Links to Organized Crime: Mexican drug-trafficking organizations and criminal groups are the primary wholesale and mid-level distributors of marijuana in the state.

WYOMING

Marijuana Situation: Marijuana is the most widely available illegal drug in Wyoming. It is readily available to users, but is less popular than methamphetamine.

Production: Cannabis is cultivated in Wyoming, mainly indoors. These grow operations are easier to conceal from law enforcement authorities and yield harvests year-round.

Indoor Domestic Grows: Typically, indoor marijuana grows are small and are located in private residences. The marijuana from these indoor grows is usually for local distribution or personal use.

---

[287] NDIC, *Wisconsin Drug Threat Assessment Update*, June 2002, citing U.S. DEA.
[http://www.usdoj.gov/ndic/pubs1/1159/marijuan.htm#Top]
[288] NDIC, *Wisconsin Drug Threat Assessment Update*, June 2002.

Outdoor Domestic Grows: Marijuana is easily grown in the remote areas of the state. Nevertheless, growers are abandoning the large outdoor cultivation sites for smaller indoor grows because they are easier to maintain and conceal from law enforcement, and because high altitudes and a short growing season also limit outdoor cannabis cultivation in Wyoming.

Processed and Imported: The majority of seized bulk marijuana is of Mexican origin, but there is a noticeable increase of seized marijuana originating in British Columbia, Canada.

Federal Drug (Marijuana) Seizures, 2002: 0 kilograms.

Major Avenues into the State: Most marijuana consumed in Wyoming is transported from Mexico. Mexican criminal groups transport large quantities of marijuana from the Southwest Border states to Wyoming. Marijuana commonly is transshipped through Arizona, California, Colorado, New Mexico, Texas, and Utah. Denver is a significant transshipment area for marijuana destined for Wyoming—both Mexico-produced marijuana and marijuana produced in California by Mexican criminal groups. Mexican criminal groups based in Denver transport wholesale quantities of marijuana to Wyoming and distribute it locally.[289]

Interstate 80 is the primary transportation route used by criminal groups to transport marijuana to and through Wyoming. Interstate 25 frequently is used. Criminal groups have also used I-90 to transport marijuana. Marijuana often is concealed inside duffel bags stowed in vehicle trunks and cargo areas. The use of hidden compartments in vehicles is not a common method of concealing marijuana in Wyoming.[290]

Links to Organized Crime: Mexican criminal groups dominate marijuana distribution at the wholesale level.[291]

II. THE DISTRICT OF COLUMBIA, U.S. TERRITORIES, AND THE COMMONWEALTH OF PUERTO RICO

AMERICAN SAMOA[292]

Marijuana Situation: Marijuana, which is widely available, is the most commonly abused illegal drug in American Samoa. However, its use does not pose the same

---

[289] NDIC, *Wyoming Drug Threat Assessment*, December 2001.
[http://www.usdoj.gov/ndic/pubs07/712/marijuan.htm#Top]
[290] NDIC, *Wyoming Drug Threat Assessment*, December 2001.
[291] NDIC, *Wyoming Drug Threat Assessment*, December 2001.
[292] NDIC, *American Samoa Drug Threat Assessment*, June 2001, Document ID: 2001-S0388AS-001.
[http://www.usdoj.gov/ndic/pubs0/674/index.htm#Contents]

problems to local authorities as methamphetamine, which has recently supplanted marijuana as the most serious drug threat in American Samoa. Although low by comparison with the U.S. national average, the level of marijuana use is disturbing to a society based on traditional Polynesian values and culture. Distributors and users barter marijuana for crystal methamphetamine and cocaine.

Production: American Samoa authorities report that cannabis cultivation is a significant local problem. A depressed local economy, weakened even more by sugar plantation closings, has increased the probability that some residents would engage in cannabis cultivation or the importation and distribution of marijuana. Most cannabis grown in the territory is for local consumption. Local authorities believe that many independent entrepreneurs cultivate cannabis and distribute marijuana on the islands. Local independent growers distribute marijuana, but tend to distribute the drug in their own areas.

Indoor Domestic Grows: No information available.

Outdoor Domestic Grows: Cannabis growers are adapting to law enforcement efforts. The growers plant crops in small patches in remote mountainous areas, which makes the plots difficult to locate and time-consuming to eradicate. Growers also use camouflage techniques to impede detection. American Samoa officials also report the presence of a hybrid plant that is denser and more difficult to detect from the air. Laws allowing forfeiture of private real estate have prompted growers to plant cannabis on public lands, such as parks, to avoid such penalties.

Processed and Imported: In addition to local cultivators, much of the marijuana in American Samoa comes from the neighboring independent nation of Western Samoa. There is no information on the distribution of marijuana from Western Samoa or other extra-territorial sources.

Federal Drug (Marijuana) Seizures, 1999-2000: During the American Samoa fiscal year 2000 (July 1, 1999, to June 30, 2000), territorial customs authorities confiscated more than 10,000 pounds of marijuana in 22 seizures at the airport and ferry terminals.

Major Avenues into the State: Criminal groups, which law enforcement officials have not identified, use cargo vessels and commercial airlines to smuggle marijuana to American Samoa. The marijuana was compacted in five plastic bags, wrapped in duct tape, and stored inside large vinyl bags. Smugglers generally conceal marijuana inside shipments of taro plants, hide it in bundles of fine mats, or mix it with dry goods and food. Drug-trafficking organizations and

criminal groups often use the mail system and cargo vessels to smuggle drugs to American
Samoa. The U.S. Postal Service (USPS) delivers mail in American Samoa. The USPS in
Honolulu screens all packages bound for American Samoa from Hawaii before handlers load the
packages onto aircraft. Drug-trafficking organizations also use cargo vessels to smuggle
marijuana from Samoa to American Samoa. The government of American Samoa is responsible
for its own customs and immigration enforcement.

Links to Organized Crime: No information available.

DISTRICT OF COLUMBIA

Marijuana Situation: Marijuana is widely available and abused in the District of Columbia. The
percentage of D.C. residents who report marijuana abuse is statistically comparable to the
percentage nationwide.[293] Marijuana, both commercial-grade and high-grade, is available in the
District of Columbia.

Production: Cannabis cultivation is very limited in the District of Columbia, primarily as a
result of its urban setting.

Indoor Domestic Grows: No information available.

Outdoor Domestic Grows: Hidden outdoor grows are increasing.[294]

Processed and Imported: Most of the marijuana available in the District of Columbia is
produced in Mexico.

Federal Drug (Marijuana) Seizures, 2002: According to FDSS, federal law enforcement
officials seized 3.6 kilograms of marijuana in 2002; however, the Metropolitan Police
Department reported seizing 59.5 kilograms.

Major Avenues into the State: Most of the marijuana available in is transported from
southwestern states, primarily by package delivery services. Additional quantities of marijuana
are transported into the District of Columbia by private and commercial vehicles and couriers
aboard commercial aircraft.

Links to Organized Crime: Jamaican and Mexican criminal groups are the principal
distributors of wholesale quantities of marijuana in the District of Columbia; however, no single

---

[293] NDIC, *District of Columbia Drug Threat Assessment Update*, May 2003.
[http://www.usdoj.gov/ndic/pubs4/4000/marijuan.htm]
[294] "Marijuana," *Pulse Check*: Trends in Drug Abuse, Office of National Drug Control Policy, November 2002.
[http://www.whitehousedrugpolicy.gov/publications/drugfact/pulsechk/]

criminal group, crew, or local independent dealer controls the majority of wholesale- or retail-level marijuana distribution in the District. Most crews that sell retail quantities of cocaine also distribute marijuana. Marijuana typically is sold at the same venues as cocaine.

GUAM[295]

Marijuana Situation: Marijuana poses a significant threat to Guam. The drug is commonly abused and readily available on Guam despite considerable law enforcement and eradication initiatives. The Guam Customs and Quarantine Authority (CQA) conducts far more investigations related to marijuana than to any other drug type. Marijuana-related offenses accounted for roughly one-fourth of adult drug-related arrests in 1999. Nevertheless, the number of marijuana-related federal sentences on Guam has been very low (none in FY2000 and only one in FY2001). Marijuana abuse by young people is a particular concern.

Production: Cannabis is cultivated both outdoors and indoors on Guam, primarily for personal consumption. Because of the poor soil, domestically produced marijuana has lower THC levels than marijuana produced in other source areas.

Indoor Domestic Grows: In order to combat local cannabis cultivation, DEA has established the DCE/SP (Domestic Cannabis Eradication/Suppression Program) on Guam.

Outdoor Domestic Grows: Violence is occasionally associated with cannabis cultivation on Guam. Law enforcement authorities encounter a significant number of small cannabis plots in remote areas, and cannabis growers occasionally booby-trap these cultivation sites, endangering both law enforcement officers and the general public.

Processed and Imported: Marijuana imported from Mexico is common.

Federal Drug (Marijuana) Seizures, 1998: In 1998, the most recent year for which data are available, law enforcement agencies seized more than 350 pounds of marijuana. The Guam CQA seized 113.79 grams of marijuana in 2001, a decrease from 9,918 grams seized in 2000.

Major Avenues into the State: Marijuana typically is smuggled into Guam from the Republic of Palau and, to a lesser extent, from Hawaii and the Federated States of Micronesia by package delivery services or in commercial air cargo. Often the relatives of Guam residents who are of Palauan descent ship large coolers containing fish or yams with 5 to 10 pounds of marijuana

---

[295] NDIC, *Guam Drug Threat Assessment*, Document ID: 2003-S0388GU-001, August 2003. [http://www.usdoj.gov/ndic/pubs4/4001/index.htm#Contents]

hidden inside the coolers' walls. Bodycarriers aboard commercial aircraft also transport marijuana into Guam. Drug-detection dogs are used as an effective measure against this method, according to DEA.

Links to Organized Crime: Wholesale distribution of marijuana is limited, and appears to be controlled by organized criminal groups. In February 2000 Guam police arrested a 35-year-old man and seized 24 bags of dried marijuana leaves worth more than $100,000 at the street level. Police believe that the man was connected to an organized crime syndicate operating from Palau.

COMMONWEALTH OF THE NORTHERN MARIANA ISLANDS

Marijuana Situation: Marijuana is readily available and commonly abused in the Commonwealth of the Northern Mariana Islands.[296] However, the extent of marijuana abuse cannot be accurately quantified because of the lack of drug abuse statistics and marijuana-related survey data for the territory. The marijuana available in the territory typically is smuggled from neighboring countries (See Figure 4). Some is produced locally; however, local production decreased from 2000 to 2001 as a result of law enforcement efforts.

Production:

Indoor Domestic Grows: Cannabis is cultivated locally in small quantities. From 2000 to 2001, law enforcement eradication efforts caused a decrease in local cannabis cultivation, and distributors had to obtain most of their marijuana from sources outside the commonwealth.

Outdoor Domestic Grows: No information available.

Processed and Imported: Most marijuana is smuggled from sources in the Philippines or the Republic of Palau.

Federal Drug (Marijuana) Seizures, 2002: n/a

Major Avenues into the State: Drugs smuggled by Filipino criminal groups into the Northern Mariana Islands often are transported by couriers aboard commercial aircraft or in air cargo, as well as in cargo containers aboard commercial maritime vessels. Individuals in the Commonwealth of the Northern Mariana Islands also use maritime vessels and package delivery services to smuggle small quantities of illicit drugs into the territory for their personal use. Criminal groups from Palau generally pay couriers to transport marijuana concealed on their

---

[296] This section is based on NDIC, *Northern Mariana Islands Drug Threat Assessment*, Document ID: 2003-S0388MP-001, October 2003.

bodies or packed in coolers. Local cultivators in the Commonwealth of the Northern Mariana Islands also transport small quantities of marijuana from island to island.

Links to Organized Crime: According to the Department of Public Safety Criminal Investigation Bureau, marijuana is transported to the Commonwealth of the Northern Mariana Islands by criminal groups that cultivate cannabis in the Philippines and the neighboring island of the Republic of Palau.

PUERTO RICO[297]

Marijuana Situation: Marijuana is one of the most widely available and commonly abused illicit drugs in Puerto Rico. According to law enforcement officials, marijuana abuse likely is much more widespread than indicated by treatment

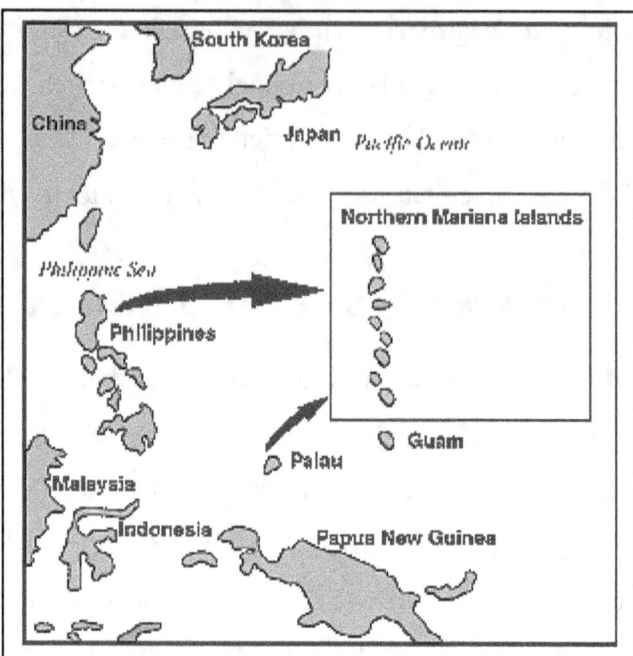

Figure 4. Marijuana Transportation from the Philippines and Palau to the Northern Mariana Islands

Source: NDIC, October 2003

admission numbers and spans most socioeconomic and age groups.

Production: Cannabis cultivation in Puerto Rico is limited.

Indoor Domestic Grows: When cannabis is cultivated in Puerto Rico, it generally is grown outdoors.

Outdoor Domestic Grows: Most of the cannabis grown in Puerto Rico is cultivated in small plots in the central mountain area and in the Rio Grande region of northeastern Puerto Rico. However, the terrain, temperature, and rainfall in Puerto Rico are not conducive to large-scale cannabis cultivation.

Processed and Imported: Most of the marijuana available in Puerto Rico is produced in Mexico. Marijuana produced locally or in Colombia or Jamaica also is available, but to a lesser extent.

---

[297] *Puerto Rico and the U.S. Virgin Islands Drug Threat Assessment*, July 2003, Document ID: 2003-S0381PR-001 http://www.usdoj.gov/ndic/pubs3/3950/

Federal Drug (Marijuana) Seizures, 1999-2002: According to FDSS data, federal law enforcement officials in Puerto Rico seized 565.4 kilograms of marijuana in 1999, 411.9 kilograms in 2000, 299.2 kilograms in 2001, and 571.1 kilograms in 2002.

Major Avenues into the State: Puerto Rican criminal groups primarily use couriers aboard commercial aircraft and package delivery services to transport Mexico-produced marijuana into Puerto Rico. Couriers, typically Puerto Rican men, generally conceal the drug on their persons or in luggage. Couriers most often transport the drug from California and Texas, often transiting U.S. cities such as Atlanta, Chicago, Dallas, Indianapolis, Orlando, Miami, Philadelphia, and Pittsburgh before arriving in Puerto Rico. Marijuana transported into Puerto Rico by package delivery services usually is mailed from California or Texas. In 2001, 331 kilograms of marijuana were seized as part of Operation Jetway in Puerto Rico. That same year, authorities seized 205 kilograms of marijuana from commercial aircraft at airports in Puerto Rico. Some of the CBP seizures may be included in Operation Jetway data.

Dominican drug-trafficking organizations and criminal groups are the primary transporters of Colombian marijuana into Puerto Rico. Colombian drug-trafficking organizations often use the transportation services of these Dominican drug-trafficking organizations and criminal groups to smuggle marijuana into the territory. These drug-trafficking organizations and criminal groups primarily transport the marijuana in small maritime vessels, including go-fast boats.

Links to Organized Crime: Puerto Rican criminal groups and local independent dealers are the principal distributors of wholesale and retail quantities of marijuana in Puerto Rico.

U.S. VIRGIN ISLANDS[298]

Marijuana Situation: Marijuana is one of the most widely available and commonly abused illicit drugs in the U.S. Virgin Islands (USVI). Marijuana abuse spans most socioeconomic and age groups.

Production:

Indoor Domestic Grows: Much less common than outdoor grows.

---

[298] *Puerto Rico and the U.S. Virgin Islands Drug Threat Assessment*, July 2003, Document ID: 2003-S0381PR-001
http://www.usdoj.gov/ndic/pubs3/3950/

Outdoor Domestic Grows: Domestically produced marijuana in the USVI is cultivated primarily outdoors; however, poor terrain and arid climate across the USVI produce a low-quality product. Nearly all the marijuana produced is intended for local distribution. Cultivation sites most commonly are located in rural areas across the islands and typically contain 100 to 200 cannabis plants.

Processed and Imported: Most marijuana available in the USVI arrives from southern island locations such as St. Lucia and St. Vincent and the Grenadines.

Federal Drug (Marijuana) Seizures, 2000-02: The DEA Caribbean Division reported the following marijuana seizures in the USVI: 0.3 kilograms in FY2000, 28.6 kilograms in FY2001, and 465.5 kilograms in FY2002.

Major Avenues into the State: Most marijuana available in the USVI arrives from southern island locations such as St. Lucia and St. Vincent and the Grenadines; however, its origin is unknown. Neither the principal transporters nor the origin of marijuana arriving in the USVI from these locations is known. Marijuana primarily is transported to the USVI in small maritime vessels.

Links to Organized Crime: In the USVI, local criminal groups and independent dealers are the primary wholesale and retail distributors of marijuana.

State	Total Cultivated Plants Eradicated	Outdoor Plots Eradicated	Outdoor Cultivated Plants Eradicated	Indoor Grows Seized	Indoor Cultivated Plants Eradicated	Bulk Processed Marijuana (in pounds)	Ditch weed Eradicated[1]
Total U.S.	3,304,760	37,926	3,068,632	2,379	236,128	25,321	569,712,725
Alabama	38,597	1,407	38,474	4	123	1,394	—
Alaska	9,128	1	86	135	9,042	48	—
Arizona	2,960	28	2,810	10	150	23	29
Arkansas	39,503	264	39,197	23	306	11	—
California	1,199,818	1,900	1,086,809	372	113,009	5,254	—
Colorado	4,170	75	1,948	20	2,222	303	134,169
Connecticut	1,320	32	1,191	2	129	3	—
Delaware	1,361	14	1,283	4	78	0	363
Florida	28,206	341	13,055	210	15,151	3,242	—
Georgia	57,534	315	56,372	27	1,162	52	—
Hawaii	525,413	11,934	525,041	7	372	139	—
Idaho	1,509	5	123	11	1,386	29	—
Illinois	32,965	422	30,961	50	2,004	608	3,098,808
Indiana	27,567	1,399	24,383	94	3,184	275	212,904,736
Iowa	1,375	17	1,036	8	339	2,730	14,520
Kansas	2,721	51	1,546	10	1,175	136	100,472
Kentucky	421,724	8,856	413,851	54	7,873	3,113	—
Louisiana	3,814	110	3,348	23	466	5	—
Maine	11,036	192	9,314	42	1,722	74	—
Maryland	4,054	122	3,670	33	384	113	—
Massachusetts	1,763	61	1,353	6	410	350	—
Michigan	32,037	154	27,135	59	4,902	244	—
Minnesota	3,552	18	1,432	42	2,120	163	4,506,438
Mississippi	10,110	163	10,080	6	30	720	—
Missouri	12,027	346	9,865	67	2,162	228	61,982,618
Montana	1,866	8	903	12	963	132	—
Nebraska	80	2	15	5	65	2	1,676,655
Nevada	7,732	9	3,593	22	4,139	272	—
New Hampshire	900	31	686	12	214	11	200
New Jersey	1,013	61	831	10	182	1,708	—
New Mexico	6,310	13	4,784	9	1,526	49	—
New York	7,664	232	6,381	37	1,283	460	470
North Carolina	89,900	1,462	88,925	18	975	205	—
North Dakota	3,860	5	3,765	5	95	5	2,755,431
Ohio	34,010	1,976	32,103	25	1,907	343	—
Oklahoma	7,928	213	2,644	130	5,284	126	—
Oregon	6,358	532	4,588	164	1,770	54	—
Pennsylvania	6,358	532	4,588	164	1,770	171.5	—
Rhode Island	156	2	32	2	124	0	—
South Carolina	9,927	122	9,228	15	699	5	—
South Dakota	3,454	2	3,420	3	34	278	263,260,015
Tennessee	479,391	2,696	477,904	14	1,487	430	—
Texas	50,110	867	40,133	94	9,977	814	712,000
Utah	1,849	6	113	7	1,736	9	—
Vermont	3,769	163	3,351	19	418	133	109
Virginia	16,170	283	13,279	54	2,891	332	0
Washington	49,246	155	23,467	216	25,779	0	—
West Virginia	36,135	564	35,287	30	848	114	2,567,110
Wisconsin	6,360	191	2,653	154	3,707	484	180,589
Wyoming	145	4	35	2	110	85	—

Table 3. Eradicated Domestic Cannabis by Plant Type, by State, 2001

— Data not available.

[1] May include tended ditch weed. Source: Drug Enforcement Administration, Office of Domestic Cannabis Eradication and Suppression Program. Unpublished data (2002).

Table 8. Total U.S. Eradicated Domestic Cannabis by Plant Type, 1989–2001
(plants in thousands)

Year	Cultivated Plants Outdoors*	Ditch weed	Cultivated Indoor Plants	Total Plants Eradicated
1989	5,636	124,289	—	129,925
1990	7,329	118,548	—	125,877
1991	5,257	133,786	283	139,326
1992	7,490	264,207	349	272,046
1993	4,049	387,942	290	392,281
1994	4,032	504,414	220	508,665
1995	3,054	370,275	243	373,572
1996	2,843	419,662	217	422,723
1997	3,827	237,140	224	241,193
1998	2,283	132,408	233	134,924
1999	3,205	130,192	208	133,605
2000	2,598	139,581	217	142,396
2001	3,069	569,713	236	573,018

—Data not available.
Note: Data for eradication supported through DEA Office of Domestic Cannabis Eradication and Suppression Program.
*May include tended ditch weed.

Source: DEA Office of Domestic Cannabis Eradication and Suppression Program, Drug Enforcement Administration, 1982–2001.

SELECTIVE BIBLIOGRAPHY

Canada. Criminal Intelligence Service Canada (CISC). "Asian-Based Organized Crime," *Annual Report on Organized Crime in Canada 2003*.
<http://www.cisc.gc.ca/AnnualReport2003/Document/CISC%202003%20Annual%20Report.pdf>

Office of National Drug Control Policy (ONDCP). Drug Policy Information Clearing House, State of Pennsylvania. *Profile of Drug Indicators*, March 2003.
<http://www.whitehousedrugpolicy.gov/statelocal/pa/pa.pdf>

Reuter, Peter. *The Mismeasurement of Illegal Drug Markets: The Implications of Its Irrelevance.*
<http://www.puaf.umd.edu/faculty/papers/reuter/pozo.pdf> In Susan Pozo, ed., *Exploring the Underground Economy: Studies of Illegal and Unreported Activity*. Kalamazoo, Michigan: W.E. Upjohn Institute for Employment Research, 1996. 172 p.

United Nations Office on Drugs and Crime (UNODC). "Cannabis," Chapter 1.1.4, *Global Illicit Drug Trends, 2003*. Vienna, Austria.

United Nations Office on Drugs and Crime (UNODC). "Trafficking in Cannabis," Chapter 1.2.4, *Global Illicit Drug Trends, 2003*. Vienna, Austria.
<http://www.unodc.org/pdf/report_2003-06-26_1.pdf>

U.S. Congress. House of Representatives. "Statement of Frank Deckert, Superintendent, Big Bend National Park Service, Department of the Interior, Before the House Government Reform Subcommittee on Criminal Justice, Drug Policy, and Human Resources, Regarding the Impact of the Drug Trade on Border Security and National Parks, April 15, 2003." <http://www.nps.gov/legal/testimony/108th/lebigben.htm>

U.S. Department of Justice. Bureau of Justice Statistics. *Sourcebook of Criminal Justice Statistics 2000, Table 4.38*, December 2001.

U.S. Department of Justice. Drug Enforcement Administration. *DEA Briefs and Background: Georgia*. <http://www.usdoj.gov/dea/pubs/states/georgia.html>

U.S. Department of Justice. Drug Enforcement Administration. *DEA Briefs and Background: New Mexico*. <http://www.usdoj.gov/dea/pubs/states/newmexico.html>

U.S. Department of Justice. Drug Enforcement Administration. DEA Public Affairs. *Drug Trafficking in the United States*, July 25, 2003.
<http://www.usdoj.gov/dea/concern/drug_trafficking.html>

U.S. Department of Justice. Drug Enforcement Administration. *Drug Intelligence Brief: The Cannabis Situation in the United States*, December 1999. <http://www.usdoj.gov/dea/pubs/intel/99028/99028.html>

U.S. Department of Justice. Drug Enforcement Administration. *Drug Intelligence Brief: Mexico Country Brief*, July 2002. <http://www.dea.gov/pubs/intel/02035/02035.html>

U.S. Department of Justice. Drug Enforcement Administration. *Drug Intelligence Brief: Money Laundering in Canada*, August 2003. <http://www.usdoj.gov/dea/pubs/intel/03034/03034.html#6>

U.S. Department of Justice. Drug Enforcement Administration. *Drug Trafficking in the United States*, September 2001.

U.S. Department of Justice. Drug Enforcement Administration. *Drug Trafficking in the United States*, October 6, 2003. <http://www.usdoj.gov/dea/concern/drug_trafficking.html>

U.S. Department of Justice. Drug Enforcement Administration. *The Mexican Heroin Trade* (DEA-20014), April 2000. <http://www.usdoj.gov/dea/pubs/intel/20014/20014.html>

U.S. Department of Justice. Drug Enforcement Administration. South America/Caribbean Strategic Intelligence Unit (NIBC) of the Office of International Intelligence, DEA Intelligence Division. The Drug Trade in Colombia: A Threat Assessment (DEA-02006), March 2002. <http://www.usdoj.gov/dea/pubs/intel/02006/index.html#6>

U.S. Department of Justice. Federal Bureau of Investigation. "FBI Wanted Fugitives," September 2002. <http://www.fbi.gov/mostwant/fugitive/sept2002/septfuentes.htm>

U.S. Department of Justice. National Drug Intelligence Center. *American Samoa Drug Threat Assessment* (Document ID: 2001-S0388AS-001), June 2001. <http://www.usdoj.gov/ndic/pubs0/674/index.htm#Contents>

U.S. Department of Justice. National Drug Intelligence Center. *California Central District Drug Threat Assessment*, May 2001. <http://www.usdoj.gov/ndic/pubs0/668/marijuan.htm#Top>

U.S. Department of Justice. National Drug Intelligence Center. *California Northern and Eastern Districts Drug Threat Assessment*, January 2001. <http://www.usdoj.gov/ndic/pubs/653/marijuan.htm#Top>

U.S. Department of Justice. National Drug Intelligence Center. *California Southern District Drug Threat Assessment* (Document ID: 2001-S0387SCA-001), May 2002. <http://www.usdoj.gov/ndic/pubs/654/index.htm#Contents>

U.S. Department of Justice. National Drug Intelligence Center. *Colorado Drug Threat Assessment Update* (Document ID: 2003-S0389CO-001), May 2003. <http://www.usdoj.gov/ndic/pubs4/4300/marijuan.htm#Top>

U.S. Department of Justice. National Drug Intelligence Center. *Connecticut Drug Threat Assessment Update*, July 2003. <http://www.usdoj.gov/ndic/pubs5/5333/marijuan.htm#Top>

U.S. Department of Justice. National Drug Intelligence Center. *Delaware Drug Threat Assessment Update* (Document ID: 2003-S0379DE-001), May 2003. <http://www.usdoj.gov/ndic/pubs4/4025/marijuan.htm#Top>

U.S. Department of Justice. National Drug Intelligence Center. *District of Columbia Drug Threat Assessment Update*, May 2003. <http://www.usdoj.gov/ndic/pubs4/4000/marijuan.htm>

U.S. Department of Justice. National Drug Intelligence Center. "Drug Transportation Across the U.S.-Canada Border," *United States-Canada Border Drug Threat Assessment* (Product No. 2002-R0423-001), December 2001. <http://www.usdoj.gov/ndic/pubs07/794/transp.htm#Top>

U.S. Department of Justice. National Drug Intelligence Center. *Florida Drug Threat Assessment Update* (Document ID: 2003-S0381FL-001), July 2003. <http://www.usdoj.gov/ndic/pubs5/5169/marijuan.htm#Top>

U.S. Department of Justice. National Drug Intelligence Center. *Guam Drug Threat Assessment* (Document ID: 2003-S0388GU-001), August 2003. <http://www.usdoj.gov/ndic/pubs4/4001/index.htm#Contents>

U.S. Department of Justice. National Drug Intelligence Center. *Illinois Drug Threat Assessment Update* (Document ID: 2002-S0382IL-001), May 2002. <http://www.usdoj.gov/ndic/pubs1/1010/marijuan.htm#Top>

U.S. Department of Justice. National Drug Intelligence Center. *Information Bulletin: Drugs, Youth, and the Internet* (Document ID: 2002-L0424-006), October 2002. <http://www.usdoj.gov/ndic/pubs2/2161/index.htm>

U.S. Department of Justice. National Drug Intelligence Center. *Intelligence Brief: National Drug Threat Assessment: Marijuana Update* (Document ID: 2002-J0403-002), August 2002. <http://www.usdoj.gov/ndic/pubs1/1335/index.htm#Overview>

U.S. Department of Justice. National Drug Intelligence Center. *Kansas Drug Threat Assessment Update*, March 2003. <http://www.usdoj.gov/ndic/pubs3/3600/marijuan.htm#Top>

U.S. Department of Justice. National Drug Intelligence Center. *Kentucky Drug Threat Assessment Update*, July 2002. <http://www.usdoj.gov/ndic/pubs1/1540/marijuan.htm#Top>>

U.S. Department of Justice. National Drug Intelligence Center. *Louisiana Drug Threat Assessment Update*, May 2001. <http://www.usdoj.gov/ndic/pubs0/666/marijuan.htm#Top>

U.S. Department of Justice. National Drug Intelligence Center. *Maine Drug Threat Assessment Update*, August 2003. <http://www.usdoj.gov/ndic/pubs5/5764/marijuan.htm#Top>

U.S. Department of Justice. National Drug Intelligence Center. "Marijuana," *Arkansas Drug Threat Assessment*, October 2003. <http://www.usdoj.gov/ndic/pubs6/6184/marijuan.htm#Top>

U.S. Department of Justice. National Drug Intelligence Center. *Marijuana Fast Facts*, March 2003. <http://www.usdoj.gov/ndic/pubs3/3593/index.htm#What>

U.S. Department of Justice. National Drug Intelligence Center. *Maryland Drug Threat Assessment Update*, August 2002. <http://www.usdoj.gov/ndic/pubs1/1827/index.htm>

U.S. Department of Justice. National Drug Intelligence Center. *Massachusetts Drug Threat Assessment Update, 2003 Update*, May 2003. <http://www.usdoj.gov/ndic/pubs3/3980/index.htm>

U.S. Department of Justice. National Drug Intelligence Center. *Minnesota Drug Threat Assessment Update,* June 2002. <http://www.usdoj.gov/ndic/pubs1/1158/marijuan.htm#Top>

U.S. Department of Justice. National Drug Intelligence Center. *National Drug Threat Assessment 2001 - The Domestic Perspective*, October 2000. <http://www.usdoj.gov/ndic/pubs/647/marijuan.htm#Top>

U.S. Department of Justice. National Drug Intelligence Center. *National Drug Threat Assessment 2002*, December 2001.
<http://www.usdoj.gov/ndic/pubs07/716/marijuan.htm#Top>

U.S. Department of Justice. National Drug Intelligence Center. *National Drug Threat Assessment 2003* (Product No. 2003-Q0317-001), January 2003.
<http://www.usdoj.gov/ndic/pubs3/3300/marijuan.htm#Top>

U.S. Department of Justice. National Drug Intelligence Center. *Nebraska Drug Threat Assessment* (Document ID: 2003-S0389NE-001), July 2003.
<http://www.usdoj.gov/ndic/pubs4/4934/index.htm>

U.S. Department of Justice. National Drug Intelligence Center. *New Hampshire Drug Threat Assessment Update*, May 2003. <http://www.usdoj.gov/ndic/pubs4/4123/marijuan.htm>

U.S. Department of Justice. National Drug Intelligence Center. *New Jersey Drug Threat Assessment Update*, August 2002.
<http://www.usdoj.gov/ndic/pubs1/1703/marijuan.htm#Top>

U.S. Department of Justice. National Drug Intelligence Center. *New Mexico Drug Threat Assessment Update*, April 2002.
<http://www.usdoj.gov/ndic/pubs07/803/marijuan.htm#Top>

U.S. Department of Justice. National Drug Intelligence Center. *New York Drug Threat Assessment*, November 2002.
<http://www.usdoj.gov/ndic/pubs2/2580/marijuan.htm#Top>>

U.S. Department of Justice. National Drug Intelligence Center. *North Carolina Drug Threat Assessment*. April 2003. <http://www.usdoj.gov/ndic/pubs3/3690/marijuan.htm#Top>

U.S. Department of Justice. National Drug Intelligence Center. *North Dakota Drug Threat Assessment*, May 2002. <http://www.usdoj.gov/ndic/pubs1/1052/marijuan.htm#Top>

U.S. Department of Justice. National Drug Intelligence Center. *Ohio Drug Threat Assessment Update*, July 2002. <http://www.usdoj.gov/ndic/pubs1/1798/marijuan.htm#Top>

U.S. Department of Justice. National Drug Intelligence Center. *Oklahoma Drug Threat Assessment*, October 2002. <http://www.usdoj.gov/ndic/pubs2/2286/marijuan.htm#Top>

U.S. Department of Justice. National Drug Intelligence Center. *Pennsylvania Drug Threat Assessment Update*, October 2003.
<http://www.usdoj.gov/ndic/pubs6/6180/marijuan.htm#Top>

U.S. Department of Justice. National Drug Intelligence Center. *Rhode Island Drug Threat Assessment Update*, July 2002.
<http://www.usdoj.gov/ndic/pubs3/3979/marijuan.htm#Top>

U.S. Department of Justice. National Drug Intelligence Center. *South Carolina Drug Threat Assessment Update*, December 2001.
<http://www.usdoj.gov/ndic/pubs07/717/marijuan.htm#Top>

U.S. Department of Justice. National Drug Intelligence Center. *State Drug Threat Assessments: Northern Mariana Islands Drug Threat Assessment* (Document ID: 2003-S0388MP-001), October 2003.

U.S. Department of Justice. National Drug Intelligence Center. *State Drug Threat Assessments: Puerto Rico and the U.S. Virgin Islands Drug Threat Assessment* (Document ID: 2003-S0381PR-001), July 2003. <http://www.usdoj.gov/ndic/pubs3/3950/>

U.S. Department of Justice. National Drug Intelligence Center. *State Threat Assessments* (undated). <http://www.usdoj.gov/ndic/topics/states.htm>

U.S. Department of Justice. National Drug Intelligence Center. *Tennessee Drug Threat Assessment Update*, May 2002.
<http://www.usdoj.gov/ndic/pubs1/1017/marijuan.htm#Top>

U.S. Department of Justice. National Drug Intelligence Center. *Texas Drug Threat Assessment* (Document ID: 2003-S0387TX-001), October 2003.
<http://www.usdoj.gov/ndic/pubs5/5624/index.htm>

U.S. Department of Justice. National Drug Intelligence Center. *United States-Canada Border Drug Threat Assessment* (Product No. 2002-R0423-001), December 2001.
<http://www.usdoj.gov/ndic/pubs07/794/transp.htm#Top>

U.S. Department of Justice. National Drug Intelligence Center (NDIC). *Utah Drug Threat Assessment*, March 2003. <http://www.usdoj.gov/ndic/pubs3/3619/marijuan.htm#Top>

U.S. Department of Justice. National Drug Intelligence Center (NDIC). *Vermont Drug Threat Assessment Update*, May 2002.
<http://www.usdoj.gov/ndic/pubs3/3999/marijuan.htm#Top>

U.S. Department of Justice. National Drug Intelligence Center (NDIC). *Virginia Drug Threat Assessment Update*, June 2003.
<http://www.usdoj.gov/ndic/pubs4/4531/marijuan.htm#Top>

U.S. Department of Justice. National Drug Intelligence Center (NDIC). *Washington Drug Threat Assessment Update*, February 2003.
<http://www.usdoj.gov/ndic/pubs3/3138/marijuan.htm#Top>

U.S. Department of Justice. National Drug Intelligence Center. *West Virginia Drug Threat Assessment*, Document ID: 2003-S0379WV-001, August 2003.

U.S. Department of Justice. National Drug Intelligence Center. *Wisconsin Drug Threat Assessment Update*, June 2002.
<http://www.usdoj.gov/ndic/pubs1/1159/marijuan.htm#Top>

U.S. Department of Justice. National Drug Intelligence Center. *Wyoming Drug Threat Assessment*, December 2001.
<http://www.usdoj.gov/ndic/pubs07/712/marijuan.htm#Top>

U.S. Department of Justice. *The Sourcebook of Criminal Justice Statistics, 2001*
<http://www.albany.edu/sourcebook>

U.S. Department of State. Bureau for International Narcotics and Law Enforcement Affairs. "Colombia," *International Narcotics Control Strategy Report, 2002*, March 2003.
<http://www.state.gov/g/inl/rls/nrcrpt/2002/html/17944.htm>

U.S. Department of State. Bureau for International Narcotics and Law Enforcement Affairs. "Jamaica," *International Narcotics Control Strategy Report, 2002*, March 2003.
<http://www.state.gov/g/inl/rls/nrcrpt/2002/html/17944.htm>

U.S. Department of State. Bureau for International Narcotics and Law Enforcement Affairs. "Mexico," *International Narcotics Control Strategy Report, 2002*, March 2003.
<http://www.state.gov/g/inl/rls/nrcrpt/2002/html/17944.htm>

U.S. Substance Abuse and Mental Health Services Administration. *Overview of Findings from the 2002 National Survey on Drug Use and Health* (Office of Applied Studies, NHSDA Series H-21, DHHS Publication No. SMA 03–3774), 2003.
<http://www.samhsa.gov/oas/nhsda/2k2nsduh/Overview/2k2Overview.htm#toc>

U.S. Substance Abuse and Mental Health Services Administration. *2002 National Survey on Drug Use and Health.* <http://www.samhsa.gov/oas/nhsda.htm>

White House. Executive Office of the President. Office of National Drug Control Policy. *Drug Facts: Marijuana*, February 2003.
<http://www.whitehousedrugpolicy.gov/drugfact/marijuana/index.html>

White House. Executive Office of the President. Office of National Drug Control Policy. *Pulse Check: Trends in Drug Abuse: Marijuana*, November 2002. http://www.whitehousedrugpolicy.gov/publications/drugfact/pulsechk/

White House. Office of National Drug Control Policy. *Drug Availability Estimates in the United States*, December 2002. <http://www.whitehousedrugpolicy.gov/publications/drugfact/drug_avail/index.html>

White House. Office of National Drug Control Policy. *High-Intensity Drug Trafficking Areas*, March 13, 2003. <http://www.whitehousedrugpolicy.gov/hidta/index.html>